THE DARKNET SUPERPACK: THE ULTIMATE ANONYMOUS COLLECTION

LANCE HENDERSON

DARKNET

How to Stay Anonymous Online
A Beginner's Guide

INTRODUCTION

"If you want total security, go to prison. There you're fed, clothed, given medical care and so on. The only thing lacking ... is freedom" - Dwight Eisenhower

Friend,

My name is Lance and I am the author of this book on encryption security and anonymity. I have been an encryption enthusiast as well as writing about security in general for over a decade. I have been a member of many security and encryption forums since the 1980s, and have been involved with computer technology long before that (yeah I know that makes me an old geezer). But if there is a security or encryption program out there, I have used it and experienced its strengths and its shortcomings and (more than likely) attracted the attention of the authorities (more on that later).

I was there when PGP first arrived on the scene and when Napster was the dominant method of p2p trading. I have used most versions of PGP, Drivecrypt, Bestcrypt, Truecrypt, Tor, Freenet, I2P and every spinoff and copycat you can think of.

Let's face it. Today we are constantly bombarded with news by the media of those trawled, raided, arrested, imprisoned, tortured and humiliated because they weren't necessarily breaking any law but because they did not know the difference between privacy and anonymity. I waited and waited for some smart hacker to put something up on Amazon to prevent this from happening.

Didn't happen.

So I decided it would be me. I stepped up to the plate pronto, though truth be told I had been meaning to put together some of the rudimentary elements of encryption security in such a way that a person without any knowledge of security encryption or anonymity could become familiar.

It is not a particularly advanced book, but rather a portal from which a beginner can step through with the assurance of anonymity when he is online. To that end I present a few tools (mostly free) at your disposal to accomplish this lofty goal. If you're an advanced user, you just might learn some hidden vulnerabilities in your favorite anonymity program.

A PhD in computer science is not required to use encryption. Neither are you required to be a programmer of any sort. You only have to know your way around your operating system and be able to follow directions to the letter. If you know how to install an operating system, or for that matter, any application at all, then you can safely use encryption programs to preserve your own digital data and safety.

PRIVACY AND ANONYMITY

If you're like one of the many billions of people on the planet who use the internet to surf the net, check email, download programs or do any kind of online work, then you probably know there are risks associated with being a habitual internet user. That's just how it is. But it is not *your* fault that there are so many latent traps and pitfalls associated with online spelunking, in whatever form that may be.

It is just a fact of life that the Good lives alongside the Evil in our lives, offline or online. This book is meant as a beginner's guide to distinguish between the Good and the Evil, and to conceal your online footprint. To be a ghost on the internet, that is our aim.

This book is not necessarily for the advanced, such as those who teach computer science courses, but rather it is for those who would like to learn to surf without compromising their identity, or having their online habits tracked 24/7, and who engage in some risky speech against their government once in a blue moon. It is also for those who might not know about some of the little known vulnerabilities in their favorite "anonymous" software programs. In the end, you just might learn there is a vast difference between "anonymity" and "privacy".

Let's start with the basics. I'll just put this out there so you know the weight of the privacy situation entirely. As of 2014, you are always being tracked on the internet in just about every way you can imagine. Search engines, cookie managers, download managers and everything you do online has the potential to make someone, somewhere, a LOT of money. Most of the time, this is because laser-targeted advertising is extremely profitable. The more they know about your habits, the more money they make.

How?

Simple. If they know more about your fears, your likes and dislikes, and how and where you spend your money, they can deliver targeted advertising to you. Laser targeted advertising. That means more power for them, less for you. Now, advertising in and of itself is not such a bad thing, but neither is a loaded gun sitting on top of the fridge. By itself it can do nothing. However it is the method of execution that defines its usefulness.

If you type any medical search term into a major search engine such as Google, Yahoo, or Bing, soon enough you'll start to see targeted ads. If you search for "how to cure a hangover", you might not see anything right away, since hangovers generally don't last that long. However if you were to type "how to cure herpes", you will likely be typing variations of that sentence over the course of a few weeks or months since it is not an easy condition to treat. Eventually you would see pay-per-click ads start to manifest themselves in your search engine results in the top corners. These ads might be selling all manner of snake-oil remedies for the cure to herpes, or they might be referrals to medical specialists.

The bottom line is this: why do they think you have this disease? The answer is because you repeatedly typed it into the search engine over the course of days/months. Over the course of a year, how much do you reveal about your medical history and identity to your favorite search engine? Do you ever wish you could keep this information private?

They like to "bubble" your identity based on how you search: the time between searches, the time of day, your country, your area. With the help of a very specific item in your internet portfolio called an IP address, they can even find out where you live, who your ISP is, and chart a course right to your very doorstep. With the help of Google Maps, and a whole plethora of other mapping applications, this can potentially lead to some very annoying and/or embarrassing situations. Do you think this information would be valuable to door-to-door salesmen? Or perhaps a company that sends out mailed advertisements? Of course.

But first things first, let's briefly say a word about the difference between privacy and anonymity since many would-be geeks confuse the two. They are not the same thing. Not by a long shot.

Anonymity & Privacy - The Differences

WHILE WE SHOULDN'T WASTE time splitting hairs here, it is probably a good idea to distinguish between the terms "privacy" and "anonymity". The two terms are not really as interchangeable as you think. Let's say that you have Firefox running, and you are working from home with a direct connection to your ISP. You don't want anyone knowing what you're doing, so you select the "private mode" tab in Firefox. This disables cookies and inhibits the ability to store any remembered websites (unless you choose to do so).

However this privacy only goes so far. It does nothing for the IP address problem we discussed earlier. Search engines still see it, as does your internet service provider. Both entities know which sites you visit and for how long, based on your IP address. In short, they can see everything. Your wife can't, however. That is why the privacy mode in web browsers were built: to keep the sites you visit private and out of the public view.

Is this privacy enough for your needs? You certainly have some level of privacy, but anonymity is another matter. Anonymity takes privacy to an entirely different level, where the IP address, and thus anything you do online, is extinguished like a wet cloth to a candle's flame through layer after layer of digital barriers. If you want to have privacy, use Firefox's private mode, or use a VPN service provider in conjunction with this feature to ensure no one else in your household can see your online footprints. This assumes that they do not have access to your laptop or PC.

If that's the case, it's game over.

If on the other hand you want anonymity, there are several tools are your disposal, one of which is to use the Tor network. In doing so, you will guarantee yourself strict anonymity and be assured of simple privacy as well, provided you don't do something stupid like blurt out enough info (on a forum, for instance) that narrows you down to a city or state.

THE ANONYMOUS TOR NETWORK

"If money is your hope for independence you will never have it. The only real security that a man will have in this world is a reserve of knowledge, experience, and ability."
   Henry Ford

Every Internet Service Provider assigns an IP address to every user who logs into their network. From there, you can connect to the millions of websites, newsgroups, and online applications that you enjoy most. IP addresses are like phone numbers. They tell your computer where to connect and send packets of data. They need this information to not only send data, such as html code, but also flash code so you can watch Youtube videos. These are targeted with ads, too. And if you bring up task manager in Windows, you can see Flash player running. Do you think Adobe is not sending data back to them about your habits? Let's continue.
   So, if the security of online privacy involves concealing the IP address between two computers, how do those two computers talk to each other without a direct connection? If you hide the phone

number, how do you make the call? The answer is simple: you have someone else in another country dial the number for you. This is the first step to being anonymous online. Do not use the IP address (yours) as a direct connection. Hire a middle man to do the talking for you. How is this possible? There are several ways. You can use the free online program called Tor, which acts a relay point between you and your online destination. There are also paid services called VPNs (virtual private networks) as well as other anonymous networks like Freenet and I2P, but we'll get into the specifics of those later.

First and foremost, let's talk about Tor.

It is the quintessential solution to online privacy since it masks your IP address. The websites you connect to have no way of knowing where you live, which ISP you are using, or what your browsing habits are. When you connect to the Tor network, you are establishing a conduit whereby if you connect to a website (Google for instance), it connects through several layers of IP addresses, or "onion layers" to reach its destination. You send out a message, email, or some type of communication. The message then goes to Bob, Jane and Herb, then finally reaches the end of the line...your favorite webpage. It routes data (backwards/forwards) through an onion later of IP addresses, so that no one adversary can see who sent what without very significant resources.

As you have probably guessed, there is a small speed hit in doing this. In order to hide your IP address, several "hops" or intermediaries, have to be jumped through. Like portals. Without going into too much technical detail, let's just say that these hops serve a very valuable purpose: to keep your private communications out of the hands of those that intend to snoop on you. Since your IP address changes every time you login to the Tor network, they can't "bubble" you effectively and target you with ads because you look like a different person from a foreign country to them each time you login. The Tor relay will end up giving you a different country to "pop-out" from with each session of your Tor browser, thus making it impossible to know your origin or where you will go next.

Let's examine an analogy between Tor and regular internet usage. You're sitting in your living room browsing anonymously via the Tor network. Your wife on the other hand is sitting in the kitchen on her Macbook, browsing without Tor. You might wonder if her browsing habits break your own anonymity. They don't...up to a point. While your isp doesn't know what *you* are doing online, they certainly do in regards to your wife.

Imagine yourself driving down Main Street in a Mercedes with tinted windows. No one can peer inside to see what you are doing at the stoplight. Not even the cops. Your wife on the other hand has non-tinted windows. People can glance over without any effort and tell if she is smoking a cigarette, listening to her iPod or talking on her phone. You are anonymous. She is not. The ISP along with any websites she visits can see everything she does online. They can't see what you are doing, however.

Firefox (and many other browsers) talk to different hosts, with the router acting as the traffic cop. An example:

Your machine: Port X, Machine A (Tor: all encrypted traffic)
Your wife: Port Y, Machine B (without Tor: all visible traffic)

It's like shooting fish in a barrel, and for the NSA, even easier than that. This same concept also applies with other things you may do on your machine while using Tor. If you use BitTorrent, your ISP can still see what you do on the P2P network even if you are running Tor simultaneously. But it cannot see the contents of the Tor network.

Thus, don't do anything on your P2P network that you wouldn't want your ISP to know about. Tor however is a different story since they cannot see what is going on between Tor relays. For all intents and purposes, Tor is like a cloak of invisibility that shields you from the sight of all onlookers, unless you have accidentally ripped a hole in the cloak (i.e. turned on javascript). If you are thinking, "Wow, it might be cool to run BitTorrent through Tor so I won't get sued". A nice goal, except BitTorrent devs aren't falling over themselves to implement this feature with Tor, and the Tor network can't really handle the bandwidth anyway. You'll just make everyone else miserable by downloading those 720p Blu-Ray rips you can easily get from Usenet (and with SSL, you're not likely to get sued.)

It might be prudent to spell out some of the best practices of using the Tor network should you decide to use it. First, although the Tor package comes with a preconfigured Firefox browser, there are still some rules you should follow that might not be apparent.

- Never give any compromising information on the Tor network that could be used to identify you. This means using your credit card for purchases, accessing your bank account, or logging into a social media site like Facebook. Card transaction are traceable. Tor, in fact, may even result in flagging transactions done via a tor exit node.
- Never mix browsers. Don't use the same browser you browse every day to Facebook and your ISP email as you do to access the Tor network. Super cookies can give away which sites you visit outside of Tor and can lead to a correlation attack on your identity/IP address.
- Always disable Javascript. The reason for this is that exploits can be utilized to reveal your IP address through using flash. Flash videos such as those on Youtube only work if this is enabled. After installation of Tor, ensure that the settings in the NoScript plugin are ON and not off by default in the plugins options screen.
- Install a bare minimum of browser plugins. You want to be as vanilla as everyone else. Too many addins, plugins, games, etc., can act as an identity beacon--fonts you use,

time of day you use certain features, can all be used to build a profile on you. BE VANILLA.
- Disable any automatic updates in the browser's options tab. This also includes updates for any addons. You should update manually, not automatically.

TOR AND TORRENTS

A word about torrents and the Tor network. It might seem on the surface that running your torrent client through the Tor network would be an obviously beneficial idea. After all, if Tor can cloak your regular Firefox downloads, surely it can do the same with torrents too, right? Well, yes and no. Yes, you could route your traffic through Tor using your favorite torrent client, however this is not a good idea for several reasons.

The first is that Tor was never developed to withstand the kind of punishing traffic bandwidth that usually comes from torrenting.

Secondly, most torrent clients like uTorrent, BitSpirit, and libTorrent are not coded properly to make you anonymous on the Tor network. They often will ignore their socks proxy settings since UDP protocol is heavily involved with torrenting, and will send your real IP address to the tracker, thereby defeating the purpose of using Tor completely. Tor in fact still does what it is coded to do: send whatever packets anonymously through the Tor network to your destination. However, it sends your IP address within the torrent tracker right along with it...anonymously.

It would be like sending a secret message in an envelope directly to the person you are attempting to hide that message from. This is not a problem with the Tor application, but rather the way torrent trackers are coded. The only fix would be if the torrent application coders themselves rewrote their applications to work harmoniously with the Tor network, something they probably will not get around to doing anytime soon (and much to the glee of Tor developers).

Tor Onion Sites

ONE OF THE most secretive elements of the Tor network is the existence of Tor Onion websites, which are pseudo top level domains acting as anonymous hidden services. In other words, they are hidden in that they can only be accessed by the Tor users themselves residing within the Tor network, rather from the open web. The motive for the creation of such hidden sites is so that the admin of the site as well as those accessing such sites cannot be traced. Since onion sites that are based on the hidden service protocol cannot be accessed from the regular internet, the address of the onion site you are looking for must be known. You can connect to an onion website on Tor just as you can a regular website, by typing the address into the address bar. For example, you might want to go to Tor2Web, in which case the address is:

http://tor2web.org/

A warning about tor2web: it is intended to offer one-sided security, that is, to protect the identity of those publishing content on Tor, not those browsing it. If you want to be secure while browsing you'll need to install the Tor application. Convenience and speed should always take a back seat where security is concerned.

Needless to say, a hidden network would not stay completely benign of nefarious webmasters if it wasn't indeed anonymous. To that end, the Hidden Wiki was developed, a singular .onion page with a wikipedia-like structure outlining in explicit detail everything from political activists to every conceivable criminal group imaginable. There are links to hundreds of various .onion sites dealing with everything from how to obtain illegal drugs, warez operations, virus creation, anonymous use of Bitcoins, illegal pornography, hacked Paypal accounts and even how to hire contract killers. Needless to say, some of these sites need to be taken with a grain of salt.

Be aware of your own country's laws regarding what can legally be obtained. What goes around in Amsterdam or Japan may not fly straight with the authorities in the USA. Remember that information that exists in Deep Web is just that: information. By itself, the information can do nothing. Words are just rearranged letters to get your point across. Pictures and videos are simply ones and zeros moving across your display. It is what they are eventually used for that define their ethics.

At the core of it, the Hidden Wiki is not terribly dissimilar from any run-of-the-mill black market operation offline. It just so happens to be online, and accessible by anyone with a little search engine sleuthing capability. Not all of the information in the Deep Web is used for nefarious purposes. Like Freenet, there are a lot of different sites that concentrate on exposing human rights abuse, political corruption, and government scandals involving high-level politicians. In the end, it is what you do with the data that determines the criminal element.

Testing your IP address visibility on Tor

WHEN YOU HAVE INSTALLED TOR, you may want to test your IP address to see if it really is broadcasting your Tor IP and not your real IP address. If you installed the default package of Tor, then Tor will show you the IP you are broadcasting as your start page. If you want to check it yourself, then go to
http://whatismyipaddress.com/.
This will show you not only your IP address, but your internet

service provider as well, and where it is located on google maps. It will also show city and country. When you are using Tor, you will see a different city/country than the one you currently reside in. Mark down what your IP address is outside of Tor, and check this site when your launch Tor if you're especially paranoid (I am).

VPNS

The last few years have seen an emergence of many different VPN (virtual private network) providers with server farms in just about every country. What a VPN does is somewhat similar to what the Tor network does. It sends a different IP address to your destination, whether that is a webpage, usenet provider, or webhost. There are some pros and cons to this. First, it is not free. A VPN will cost the same amount you would get for Usenet service: about ten dollars per month. This amount fluctuates from provider to provider. Sometimes it is a little more, sometimes a bit less, but all providers have you login to their service the same way you would an ISP. Most of the configuration is automatic and doesn't require any technical wizardry to setup. Five minutes, give or take.

Another major difference is that while Tor provides anonymity, and is free, a VPN will provide you with *privacy*, but not necessarily *anonymity*. This is because the middle man, the VPN in this case, knows your real IP address. They have to know this information in order to forward your requests. The VPN service is built upon a different technology than Tor. It is built for *speed* and *stability*. Torrenting, you say? Knock yourself out.

Further, let's say that you're a Chinese dissident. You don't like the way your country is headed in regards to free speech and human rights. You can't exactly criticize the Chinese government in the Saturday paper can you? Of course not. So what is a good, law-abiding dissident to do? You build a news website using a VPN in another country and relay your dissent through that internet portal. You don't necessarily have to build a website. You could simply setup your newsreader to access Usenet via the VPN connection. In that way, the Chinese government could not determine the origin of any anti-governmental messages through the use of the IP address (unless of course you hint of incriminating personal information that narrows down your location).

You can also access forbidden places by the Chinese government, such as Facebook, Skype, private chat rooms and even Usenet. The reason these kinds of places are blocked by the Great Firewall of China is precisely because they are fertile ground for free speech enthusiasts. While this may sound like an easy way to circumvent the Chinese police, remember that most VPN providers offer connections through almost every civilized country you can think of. If you are a Chinese dissident, I wouldn't connect to a VPN located in China, but rather Canada or perhaps a country hostile to China. Most VPN providers offer a selection of many servers to choose from in which to route your messages and traffic.

On that note, let's talk a bit about law enforcement and VPNs. Many in the past have erroneously thought that a VPN carried with it a strong dose of anonymity, similar to what Tor offered. It doesn't quite stack up that way. A VPN service offers privacy, not anonymity, as we stated. They do not route your data through intermediaries the way Tor does. Depending on which VPN you choose, you could end up with one in Switzerland who will not cave to anyone's request for subscriber information outside of Sweden. On the other hand, you might have a US based provider who will bow down to the whims of any judge's warrant for subscriber information in a New York minute.

While most are perfectly safe for purposes of torrents and the like, one should think twice about using a VPN in a western country for felonious offenses, as they will most likely give your name and address up to law enforcement in order to stave off any fines and/or trouble by the government. There are of course ways around this, such as not using your credit card and paying anonymously, however sometimes it is better not to use a VPN at all for those kinds of purposes (think hackers, smuggling, illicit banned goods, drugs etc). Vpns have never been built with anonymity in mind. Tread carefully.

TOR RELAYS

"Who can you trust? Nobody, cause nobody wants you here."

Those words, uttered by Sean Connery in The Untouchables, are as appropriate for darknet discussions as they are for the mob. But let's be realistic for a moment. There are, as you read this, ten thousand more organized crime syndicates spread out over the net than you will ever come across in the "Deep Web". They run the same secure, enterprise-grade software that Wall Street banks use and cloak themselves better than Ringwraiths. No outside eyes peer in unless the alphabet agency has a guy on the inside. Cartels like these rake in millions in drugs, arms, counterfeit pharmaceuticals, mercs and excel at human trafficking.

The Deep Web is similar, but not that similar. But those who are for outlawing it completely are really advocating for more control rather than for less crime, as was the case with Prohibition. They claim the negatives outweigh the positives. Let's say a guy in North Korea gets curious as to why his government is censoring information from him. He wants to know why. So he uses Tor to access websites blocked by the North Korean regime (Facebook for instance, to hook up with an uncle who may have escaped to S. Korea). And he does so anonymously. So that is one positive trait.

But this, they say, does not outweigh the child porn, contract killers and heroin runners. They say, people aren't going to Tor to discuss ways of avoiding the mine fields on the border and neither are they discussing the latest enlightenment from Tibet. Yes, anonymity has its meritorious moments, but someone who wants to hide almost always does so at the circumvention of the law. There are only so many North Koreans, after all.

They assume, quite wrongly, that those criminals engaged in the above activities would cease to exist. They are wrong. These were around before Tor and the Deep Web were even a spark in the developer's minds, and will thrive regardless of what government regulations are cooked up by congress critters. The same as it was during Prohibition.

Hazards of running a Tor Exit Node

In 2012, an Austrian named William Weber, an IT admin, was arrested for running Tor servers that route anonymous traffic over the Tor network. The charge? Distributing illegal images. Police detected the data coming off one of the nodes he ran. A police raid ensued. Searched his home. Confiscated his Xbox, iPods, all drives and miscellaneous electronics and even his legally owned firearms. The court order revealed one of the Tor exit nodes (he ran seven) was transporting the data.

Notice, we did not state that *he* transported the data. The data in question is going to come down on some node, be it his or someone else's. That is how Tor works: via encrypted traffic that gets piped through servers on its own IP address, through various layers (hence the term Onion layer) and decrypted back into its initial form. An ISP cannot discern the contents in transit. However, law enforcement can see the contents coming out of a node that was sent from the other side of the globe. Holding a Tor node operator responsible would be like holding a forum administrator responsible because some anonymous poster said he was going to kill the president.

Misuse of Tor end nodes are fairly common. Back in 2008, a man was arrested by German police after bomb threats passed through his Tor node, and similarly, they confiscated all electronics--hardware, software, and threatened imprisonment because someone abused his generosity. These kinds of cases bring up a few parallels. Should the Austrian government sue Google for having illegal data flowing through its servers? We're not only talking about images or bomb threats. Warez, kidnapping, extortion, bribery, espionage, a long laundry list of crimes occur on a daily basis via their search engine, and though Google cooperates with law enforcement (as Weber did), when was the last time you heard Google's servers confiscated by a court order?

And then there is encryption. Should Drivecrypt and Truecrypt developers be held liable for helping illegal enterprises? Truecrypt is a software used quite heavily by Mexican cartels as well as organized crime in the United States. Law enforcement, particularly the FBI, tends to shoot first and ask questions later. Maybe. If they're in a good mood (or ordered to by a judge). Meanwhile, your electronics are confiscated and your reputation damaged.

The entire ordeal has been setting dangerous precedent for years, as any average Joe who just happens to pass some part of an illegal data packet through his connection (or unsecured WiFi) can be prosecuted. Furthermore, police are not known for their technical aptitude, in Austria or anywhere else. They took his Xbox360 and anything else plugged in that looked about as complex as a toaster. We mustn't allow Tor node operators to be scapegoats. If Tor dies, innocent people die. They won't get the word out about corrupt government actions without risking their own lives. And they shouldn't *have* to risk anything to get the word out.

As of 2014, no one has been sued or prosecuted in a U.S. court of law for running a Tor relay (unlike those using BitTorrent). Furthermore, using Tor as well as running a Tor relay is perfectly legal under U.S. law.

Benefits of Running a Tor Exit Node

We've talked a little about the risks of being a Tor exit mode. You might be saying, well, the risks far outweigh the benefits. And in some places, you're right. But it depends on where you live, the laws, the bandwidth, your setup, etc.

So what are the benefits?

- Help people all over the world browse the net anonymously (esp. censorship-prone countries)
- Provide support for the network
- Exit nodes are always scarce. Your generosity supports development.
- Defeat tyranny (what's that? Well, North Korea for one)
- Prevent websites/search engines from tracking you
- Help others get beyond the Great Firewall of China
- Join the Rebel Alliance (yeah right)

At this point it might be prudent to relay my own experience. The first time I used Tor, I was already fairly good as not only admin of several websites and hosted machines, but quite good at encryption. My frame of thought was, if I was no slouch at encryption, Tor would be a piece of cake. And it was...for a while. I had plenty of bandwidth available, so I jumped right in.

Being in North America at the time, it would be a few weeks to get up to speed on all the pros and cons of Tor relays, and not from the technical standpoint, but the legal. I envisioned Blackhawk helicopters and car chases involving white vans with license plates that read "NOTOJ" should I be so unlucky to screw up my configuration. Putting my paranoia aside, I finally got it running full speed, and studied the network logs like a hawk to see what it was doing. And I was well-pleased. Full of pride, you might say.

Tor traffic trickled in like a sprinkle before a storm, and after three days my node had spread just as the bandwidth limits I had preset kicked in. The feeling was euphoric. Addicting. I envisioned some tech-starved villager in North Korea accessing something verboten by the Korean government. I kept thinking about Matthew Broderick in WarGames and the famous line, "The only way to win the game, was not to play." Well, I tweaked it to add, "...by the Man's rules." It was all good.

Until a week later when my ISP ordered me to cut the Tor umbilical. It was polite, but stern. It seemed a few complaints sailed their way. As my luck would have it, that North Korean villager turned out to be a swarm of torrentors using Tor to evade the trackers setup by the record industry. It hampered Tor's bandwidth like a hurricane had set upon it.

"Torrents?" I said. "Really?"

Yes indeed. And even though I lived in Canada at the time and wasn't worried about a torrent of lawsuits, I still did not want other Tor users to be hindered by greedy users. The problem I ran into was that filtering torrent traffic is a bit counterproductive since BitTorrent is able to run on any standard port. I tried blocking ports 80 and 443 (web traffic). It wasn't a silver bullet, however, since torrent users could still use other ports. BitTorrent clients like uTorrent and BitLord can run on any port, almost all randomly chosen. Thus every port you add to your exit node can connect to another client listening on that same port. Some users even enable a range of ports, thereby increasing the chance of getting a DMCA takedown for you.

Hence, we come to the Reduced Exit Policy of Tor, an alternative to the default exit policy. You are still able to connect and at the same time block TCP ports (usually) used by BitTorrent users. Below are a couple of port lists to check against BitTorrent clients:

https://secure.wikimedia.org/wikipedia/en/wiki/List_of_TCP_and_UDP_port_numbers

http://www.speedguide.net/ports.php

What should become clear as crystal at this point is that you should not run an exit relay from your house, with emphasis on *should not*. Why not? Because of the aforementioned scenarios with law enforcement. As we've seen in prior cases, it is quite easy for them to get a judge's signature (a judge who knows squat about Tor) on a no-knock warrant in the USA should they start sniffing your traffic. Not only will they take your computer, but everything with connectivity, which these days includes TVs and monitors. Much better to run the exit relay from a commercial provider (and there are many). A few in the U.S. who are not only knowledgeable about Tor, but have the support needed to deal with abuse cases are as follows:

Amazon Web Services (AWS)
    AmeriNOC
    Arvixe
    Axigy
    ChunkHost
    Team Cinipac
    Cyberonic
    Ethr.net
    Evolucix
    Future Hosting

A full comprehensive list is available at the Tor Wiki that covers many countries, each with their own subset of laws dealing with anonymity services (and extensive comments on each).

https://trac.torproject.org/projects/tor/wiki/doc/GoodBadISPs

In the event you do decide to run a Tor relay from home however, make sure you inform your ISP and ascertain whether you have their full support (i.e. no surprises a month down the line). The abuse complaints will come sooner or later, just as they did for me. The Tor forums have a list of ISPs that are friendly towards Tor and are knowledgeable about the network, in addition to ones that are not.

FREENET

Freenet is unlike any other anonymizing beast on the entire internet. It takes quite a wizardly mind to crack its protection and to that, it is a bit like chess: easy to grasp the basics, long and difficult to become a master. Built in 2000, Freenet is a vast, encrypted datastore spanning thousands of connected computers across the globe, all distributing encrypted contents from one computer to another. To this end, it is somewhat similar to a P2P program like Emule. Except with eEule, every file, whether it mp3, rar or iso is out there in the open for weeks, months and years, along with the IP addresses, trumpeting who downloaded and uploaded every file. You know what you upload, and what you download, and so does everyone else.

Freenet is different in this regard.

While your IP address is visible, what you are uploading out of your datastore is not. You initially setup the size of the datastore for others to download from you. This datastore is encrypted. You have no idea what will eventually be inside, as the contents are encrypted. It is a bit like a postal worker delivering the mail. He has no idea what is in the package he is delivering. That is not his job. His job is to deliver the contents to its destination. Therein is the strength of Freenet.

While you can see your downloads merrily trickle their way down to your laptop, there is no way to decrypt your datastore's content and see what it is you're passing along to the nearest node. And to that, the bigger the datastore, the more efficiently Freenet runs. After one inserts a file into Freenet, the user is free to shutdown their pc. This is unlike torrents in that the stability of the torrent file is dependent on the length of online seeds. Thus, high reliability is a factor with Freenet files, as the file is spread between encrypted blocks residing in the Freenet system.

Freenet is slow. So slow in fact, that you may not see any measurable progress in download speed for a couple hours or so after install, and it may be a day before you can see extensive progress with old (unpopular) files. Don't get discouraged because of this. It will speed up gradually over time.

Now, with your IP address out there in the open, you might be tempted to think it is not very anonymous. Nothing could be further from the truth. Whatever you download is encrypted from one end of Freenet to the other, and decrypted on your PC. No one looking in from the outside can see who requested which file or message. No one on the inside knows either, except you. For this reason alone, it is extremely censorship-resistant. This level of anonymity requires each node that requests data to operate in "hops", from many intermediaries, similar to what you would see in Tor.

However, no node knows who requested which file, thus giving a high level of anonymity. This requirement carries a price in that downloads as well as uploads are initially extremely slow, especially for new data inserts.

Let's say you want to share an iso dvd image on this network. You fire up Frost (a front-end addon for Freenet), then hit insert, then select the file. Then depending on how big your file is, you could be waiting for a long time, say several hours, for the file to finish. If this file had been inserted three months prior, and was very popular, with dozens of users trying to fetch said file, then that file would download very fast. However this is not usually the case with new files since every kernel of data on Freenet operates faster if and only if it is a popular file.

There are two types of security protocols that Freenet offers: Darknet and Openet. For Openet, you connect to other users, called "strangers". There is nothing sinister about this, as this is what the Freenet developers envisioned that most beginners would use. The IP address of said strangers is visible, but the anonymity of Freenet isn't nested in the security of the IP address like Tor, but rather it is nested in the encryption methods of the distributed datastore.

The other security option, which you are given at installation, is Darknet, where you will connect to "friends" rather than "strangers". These will be Freenet users that you will have (presumably) previously exchanged node references, which are public security keys. With Darknet mode, it is assumed that you will have a higher level of trust, as your node reference is related to your online Freenet identity. Needless to say, this mode is not to be taken lightly. You really do have to TRUST those you add to this protocol. That is, the darknet protocol.

Within Freenet, there are no censors. Every kind of free speech is allowable and often encouraged. The very way in which Freenet is programmed makes it impossible to remove any message from the system by a censor. Individual users may opt to erase certain comments from the frost system, for instance, but this is only at the local level, on their machine, and not the Freenet network itself. Thus, no religious group for instance can force others in the network to conform to their belief and discussion system. No one on Freenet may deem information so offensive that it must be removed. Not even Freenet developers.

Needless to say, this has some negative consequences in that anyone may say anything to anyone at any time. Some Freesites on the Freenet network are plagued by spammers, identity thieves, terrorists, molesters, government anarchists and software pirates. The

Freenet developers have stated this is a necessary evil of sorts in allowing 100% free speech to reign free. It could be argued that one should not allow illicit digital goods to be exchanged between users just so people could speak freely, however one of the stated purposes of Freenet is to preserve such a system in the even of societal collapse or oppression.

While there are no rules to govern Freenet by in the sense of censoring unsightly posts, a few guidelines have been posted in scattered parts of Freenet that should probably be heeded:

1.) NEVER GIVE anyone on Freenet your node-reference, as this contains information that could be exploited to correlate your Freenet identity with your IP address.

2.) Same rule as Usenet: Don't give in to trolling activity. Trolling by its very nature flourishes with the more responses it receives. Ignore them.

3.) Never give out any personal info: your location, where you grew up, which restaurants you like most, what kinds of clothing stores you shop at, as these could zero-in on your location

4.) Take notice of different regionally spelled words (labor vs. labour, color vs. colour: these could reveal your home country).

5.) Never use any nickname that is the very same unique nickname you use for opennet forums. Use popular nicknames like Shadow, John, Peter and the like.

THE HIGHEST SECURITY setting can be a bit foreboding, but perhaps necessary in countries where criticizing the government could land you a lifetime in a work camp. It has an encrypted password option to encrypt Freenet usage. This setting is in the security configuration, along with a host of other options of varying system requirements. The higher the security setting, the slower Freenet will run as it will use more resources to cover your footsteps.

When first installing Freenet, it will likely take no more than a few minutes, while asking you which security level you would like to operate at (normal up to maximum). After that and a bit of time allowed for Freenet to find nodes to connect to, you'll be presented with a previously hidden world where a Freenet index lists every possible combination of Freesites available. Everything from anarchy sites to Iranian news, to pirated copies of books, films and game roms and even a few political how to documents describing how to protest a corrupt government without getting caught will be indexed.

These are the types of things typically either censored by Google in China, or deindexed altogether. The only thing missing is a disclaimer at the bottom of the screen welcoming you to the deepest, darkest depths of the internet, known as Darknet.

Optionally, you may run Freenet from an encrypted Truecrypt container file. You will need to create a Truecrypt volume that is sufficiently large enough to hold whatever files you intend on downloading from Freenet. Remember to keep in mind that when Freenet asks you how large you want the datastore to be, the size you choose could be a benefit to other Freenet users. The larger the datastore, the more efficient the Freenet network operates.

That is not to say that downloads will *always* come down faster, but rather encrypted data will last longer on the network. This is similar to the retention times that Usenet providers talk about when they try to sell their servers to you. The higher the data retention, the longer the files on the network will last. There is also another bonus to having a large datastore, say fifty gigabytes or so. Files that you may request may already be in your datastore after having run Freenet for some time, thereby shortening the time to retrieve them.

With your Truecrypt container you can run Freenet with the volume mounted and not worry about your Freenet activities being used against you in case of your computer being confiscated. You can also do the same for your Tor browser as well. Install Tor browser bundle to a mounted Truecrypt container and only run the program when mounted.

Frost

FROST IS a separate application than Freenet, which acts as a front-end. It makes browsing on the Freenet network more akin to browsing Usenet newsgroups. Download at:

HTTP://JTCFROST.SOURCEFORGE.NET

AFTER RUNNING FREENET, you can optionally run Frost simultaneously to download inserts from the Freenet network. It is not mandatory but it is incredibly helpful. Run Freenet, then Frost, and then wait an hour or so for Frost to find some groups, and then hit the globe button at the top panel to subscribe to groups. These groups all have discussions going about every topic under the sun. Some of them are fairly dead, with almost no discussion at all, and others swarm with activity.

Frosty Tips

1.) If you started downloading something in Frost, finish it in Frost

2.) Like Usenet, don't troll the boards. It will get you put on user's "ignore" list and they will henceforth not see any messages from your nick.

3.) Never reveal your node reference to anyone on the Frost boards, as it could be used to locate you.

4.) Set days to download backwards to 60 (or however long you wish). Just be aware that it may take several days to retrieve all messages if you select a very large amount of days.

5.) In the options/preferences tab, you may adjust the setting to ignore comments from users with less than four messages attached to their nickname. This is very effective at eliminating most spam messages on the board.

TRUECRYPT, VERACRYPT, ETC.

There are two types of encryption: one that will prevent your sister from reading your diary and one that will prevent your government. - Bruce Schneier

IT WOULD BE FOLLY if we went to all this work of laying out the security options to keep our online footprint out of nefarious hands and not say something about our offline footprint. Put simply, you should tread carefully with your offline habits just as you should your online persona.

    Let's say you're in your favorite cafe. You're sipping your ice cappuccino with your laptop in the corner of the coffee scented shop and have to make a break for the restroom. It'll only take a minute or so, right? While you're in there, the guy sitting at the next table decided to insert a USB key into your laptop and upload a keylogger virus into your machine. This keylogger is ridiculously small in size, and can hide undetected by most users. It can even disguise itself as a windows service and look just like any other svchost process, all the while taking snapshots of your screen, recording everything you typed for the remainder of that day, and emailing them to whomever installed the virus.

You would be a bit worried if you knew about it.

However, most don't realize they leave themselves vulnerable to such attacks in public places. Some experts have referred to this as the "evil maid attack", after a scenario whereby you are in a hotel and briefly step outside for a moment and at which point the maid comes in and has physical access to your running machine. They now have access to every cookie stored by your browser in addition to any credit card numbers you have used, possible phone numbers/emails of friends, and the like. How to prevent this?

For starters, to prevent identity theft you need to seriously consider full-disk encryption. This is not nearly as complex as you might think. It is ridiculously easy encrypt your boot drive and costs you nothing, and potentially saves you from months of headache.

There are several encryption apps at your disposal: the paid programs, such as PGP, Drivecrypt, and Phonecrypt, and the popular free versions, PGP and Truecrypt. There are a few differences between them but the one thing to take away from both free and paid versions is that they prohibit anyone from booting your computer, laptop, or phone without the password.

Truecrypt is free, and does this by creating a 256 AES encryption key. You install the application, select your drive you want to encrypt, and select your passphrase and create an encrypted key. Simple.

How does this benefit you? Well, the next time that thief who stole your laptop tries to boot up the hard drive, without the password he'll be out of luck. He is presented with this password field before windows even boots, and if it is not keyed in correctly, the drive halts. The password, if sufficiently long, is enough to withstand almost any brute-force attack, even by the NSA. Just make sure to use a passphrase that will be easy to remember, but long enough to thwart any attacker: 15-character passphrase with upper/lowercase letters with a number or two.

Just how strong is Truecrypt? It is considered impossible to crack, on the order of millions of years. It would take quantum computers eons to crack even a moderately length passphrase using brute-force methods. In all likelihood the absolute weakest link is *you*.

Keyloggers can obtain your password if you are unlucky enough to get one. However, these are a fairly rare occurrence if you keep your operating system, anti-virus and anti-malware programs up to date. The other weakest link is your passphrase. You would be surprised at just how many people use their own personal information in their passphrases. Doing this might make the password easier to remember, but also easier to crack.

A good passphrase is made up of lower and upper case characters in addition to spaces, which lend more entropy bits to the protection. At each instance a bit is added to a passphrase, the computational crunching requirement to crack such passphrase is doubled. If I were living in North Korea or China, for example, I would seriously consider a passphrase that was at least twenty characters long, with some keyboard symbols thrown in for good measure. Most people do not like to remember a twenty character passphrase however, so they use a less random one.

Drivecrypt is another encryption program, but it is not open-source and is not free. I have used this program for eight years and have to say if money is a concern, then go with Truecrypt as it has many of the same functions that Truecrypt does, and for zero cost. Drivecrypt has an option called "bootauth" which is short for boot authorization. The install process is similar to Truecrypt, though the bootup passphrase screen is a little different. You boot your hard drive, and then type in the passphrase to boot the OS. Truecrypt has this function as well.

As stated, it is not open-source. What that means is that it cannot be studied by the public sector (read: security users) to determine if any backdoors have been coded in. Like Truecrypt, it offers the option to create an encrypted operating system that holds a hidden operating system as well whose existence can be denied to those trying to harm or prosecute you. This is especially beneficial if you live in the UK, where failure to hand over a passphrase to an encrypted hard drive can get you two years in prison on a contempt of court charge. However you could give them the password to your decoy system. There is no way they could know if you were concealing a hidden operating system without a keylogger in place.

Truecrypt and Drivecrypt give no hints or leak any data regarding the existence of hidden files. The only way to mount said file is to know the password, and there are two you create with such an option: one for the decoy, and one for the hidden container/operating system.

Truecrypt and Drivecrypt also support the use of encrypted container files, which when clicked will mount the file the same way a mounting application like DaemonTools or Nero mounts an iso image. Prior to mounting, the application will ask you for the password. Mistype the password and the container does not mount at all. This can be very handy as there are a plethora of private items that you could conceal from government or any kind of prosecuting institution, such as medical records, tax records, school transcripts, business correspondence and the like.

Veracrypt may also be an option if you don't mind the Truecrypt interface. In fact, they look and act very similar.

VeraCrypt main features:
- Creates a **virtual encrypted disk** within a file and mounts it as a real disk.
- Encrypts an **entire partition or storage device** such as USB flash drive or hard drive.
- Encrypts a **partition or drive where Windows is installed** (pre-boot authentication).
- Encryption is **automatic**, **real-time**(on-the-fly) and **transparent**.
- Parallelization and pipelining allow data to be read and written as fast as if the drive was not encrypted.
- Encryption can be hardware-accelerated on modern processors.

- Provides **plausible deniability**, in case an adversary forces you to reveal the password: **Hidden volume** (steganography) and **hidden operating system**.

SOME TIPS FOR TRUECRYPT/VERACRYPT users:

1.) If you have one, disable the firewire port, as this can be used to reveal the encryption keys.

2.) Never leave any containers mounted on a laptop when crossing a border station, unless you want your private information in said container to be shared with the guards.

3.) Never leave your PC powered on and unattended for any lengthy amount of time (public wifi spots, cafes, libraries, college classrooms, etc). All security goes out the window when an attacker (or anyone else) has physical access to your machine. Neither Truecrypt nor Drivecrypt can protect your data in such a case, as the attacker can install a keylogger that can record your keystrokes.

Thumbnails

IF YOU POSSESS any incriminating snapshots (flings, Wikileak photos, informant docs) then at a later time delete the images in the folder, be aware that a shadow copy still exists. In windows XP (yes, legions of users are still clinging to this OS), thumbnails of jpegs are stored within each folder of the image's location. So if you have a folder called "government office snapshots", you will have thumbnails enabled in the folder settings tab for any pictures (jpegs, bitmaps, etc), and a hidden thumbs.db file will be present that shows a mini version of the picture in question. So even if you delete the jpegs, this hidden file will still reveal to anyone what the contents of the original folder were.

The only way to see or disable this hidden file is to go to Tools – Options – View and set the option to "show hidden files and folders".

Until this is done, every single folder with pictures in it will store a mini-snapshot of the pictures unless this is disabled. Windows 7 is a completely different file system to Windows XP. Instead of keeping the thumbnail cache within the folder where the pictures reside, it stores it in a central location (%userprofile%\AppData\Local\Microsoft\Windows\Explorer)

I HAVE FOUND it much better to just leave the thumbnail option off in Windows 7, as the images load fairly quickly without the need for a cache to speed things up. There are other files, like text, audio and the like, that are also at risk of being discovered if you do not take precautions to securely delete the file. That does not mean deleted from the *recycle bin*, however. When you delete any items from the recycle bin, all that does is tell the operating system that the space previously occupied by that file can be written to again. It does not delete the file permanently until that space is overwritten to again by some other program.

Government agencies have programs that can *undelete* a file. The way around this is to use various programs to securely delete a file, such as Ccleaner. This app has an interesting wipe utility as well, in that it can wipe the free space of any previously deleted contents on the hard drive. You can even do this while the operating system is in use.

Needless to say, if you have a 2 terabyte hard drive and you're only using 20% of the drive, with 80% being "free space", then it will be a few hours for it to finish the wipe process, dependent on the speed of the hard drive and what other programs you have running. It does not touch any installed programs that exist already on the system unless you tell it to, and then only that free space that is allocated for use.

Swap File

LET'S TALK briefly about the "swap" file that most operating systems use. What this means is that sometimes during heavy PC usage, you will run low on system memory, and then the operating system will use your hard drive as a temporary ram storage device. This is what is called the "swap file", which increases the speed of computer operations. This swap file can be a veritable gold mine of data to someone with nefarious intentions.

Text files, video thumbnails, and word document fragments can exist herein, enough to print out a pretty good snapshot of your past. There have even been court cases where people were convicted in court using nothing but thumbnail fragments.

You can disable the swap file windows uses by going to control panel, System & Security, System, Advanced, Performance, Settings, Advanced, Virtual Memory and click Change. Choose "No Paging File". Reboot.

Note: Some resource intensive games use the swap file to speed up their games when there is not enough ram. If you run into any slowdowns with normal PC usage you can always switch this option back on, then reboot.

I2P

I2P, otherwise known as the "Invisible Internet Project" is another option that people can use to hide their online IP address. It shares a lot of the same characteristics of other networks in that it routes traffic through neighboring peers. The developers have stated that their main goal is not necessarily one of 100% anonymity (a goal some say is impossible), but rather to make the system too troubling and expensive to attack from the outside. It is an *anonymizing* network with several layers of encryption wrapped around all the data that travels through the system.

I2P VS Tor

YOU MIGHT THINK this sounds a lot like Freenet, but the similarity is actually more like Tor's network. I2P offers interactivity with websites, blogs, forums, chat, search engines and all without the need to install any of them locally. Such are the hallmarks of I2P. Websites that exist in the I2P network are called Eepsites, and are hosted anonymously with I2P being a strict requirement to access these websites. In that vein, it is similar to the .onion sites accessible only via Tor. Every PC that is connected to the I2P network shares in the forwarding of encrypted packets of data through proxies prior to the final destination. Each *subsequent* proxy prunes a layer of encryption at various intervals until encryption is removed. The bottom line is this: No one knows the origin of said packets, a trait also shared by Tor. While it is true that both Tor and I2P have different goals in mind, there exists many similarities:

- Both exist as anonymizing networks
- Both use layered encryption to funnel data
- Both have hidden services
- Tor has Exit Nodes and I2P has Outproxies

Benefits of Tor over I2P

- LARGER USER BASE THAN I2P; support from academic sources, constant improvements in stability and resistance to attacks
    - Funding is sourced from many countries around the globe
    - Large number of Exit Nodes
    - Translated into many languages
    - Optimized for Exit Traffic
    - Memory more optimized than I2P
    - Written in C

Benefits of I2P over Tor

- HIDDEN SERVICES much faster than the Tor network.
    - Not as many DOS (denial of service) attacks as Tor.
    - Compatible with peer-to-peer file sharing (Tor is not).
    - Tor tunnels last a long time compared to I2P. This ensures less attacks as the number of samples a hacker may use are limited.
    - Every peer routes data for others.

- Offers TCP/UDP.
- Written in Java.

AS YOU CAN SEE, both networks are safe enough for anonymity, as long as you aren't a world-hunted target. To this, a user's anonymity is typically broken due to their own sloppy behavior--their overconfidence being the weakest link in most cases (using the same login names on many websites, mixing these with Tor and non-Tor websites, and enabling JavaScript/Flash).

Since I2P is not built to act as a proxy to the WWW, you should use Tor if you want to surf anonymously. The outproxies on I2P, as you've probably guessed, are similar to the exit nodes on Tor, but they do not have the greatest support and tend to be unstable. Thus you should use Tor for anonymous web browsing and I2P for I2p eepsites. One option is to use Foxy Proxy to test it yourself. Be aware however that since there are fewer outproxies than Tor exit nodes, it may be easier for an adversary to identify your activities. It all depends on how much risk you want to assume and what the ramifications are if you are caught (and in which country).

You can also use I2P for BitTorrent and iMule as well as other P2P applications. Like Freenet, you will find that I2P will grow in speed the longer you use it without interruption. Torrents will be faster. Data will come down like lightning. Tor users will thank you for it. There are already too many torrent users on Tor that clog the network and make it difficult for people in dire straits who need anonymity for their political actions far more than the next Incubus CD.

While I2P is a technical powerhouse for anonymity, it can be a bit like a house of cards. Once the Ace is pulled from the bottom layer (by you), it can be rendered moot. I2P is just a tool, as is Tor and Freenet. It is not an invisibility cloak. Do something stupid, like move too much when a pack of Orcs are looking your way, you're bound to get an arrow in a place where you least expect it. Thus, act smart by being proactive in anonymity:

1.) TURN OFF JAVASCRIPT

Yes, it bears repeating, with arms waving in the air and shouting at the top of our lungs. Javascript is the bane of not only Tor, but other networks that rely on cloaking your IP address. Leaving this beastly plugin ON allows code to be run on your machine, code that will decloak you. Look at your browser settings and disable it. Also disable cookies. Super cookies are deployed in the wild to track down Tor users. Don't let it happen to you on I2P. Javascript can reveal a ton of metrics that fingerprint a user. Display resolution, page width, font and so on can be sent to an adversary by stealth. If you're in doubt, take a look at the web API at Mozilla:

HTTPS://DEVELOPER.MOZILLA.ORG/EN-US/DOCS/WEB/API

2.) SILENCE IS GOLDEN!

DON'T SAY A PEEP. Sure, you can talk. But refrain from discussing: the weather, your geography, your hobbies, your city politician that was just arrested for soliciting hookers. If someone says, "Hows the weather in your town?" You say: "Sunny." Every time. Alternatively, you may misinform. The CIA does it, why can't you? Their entire organization is built on secrecy and deception. Don't get too choked up about a few white lies. Spreading misinformation about trivial things like the weather and the local politics can really put a nail in an adversary's coffin. Ditto on employment. If you are asked about your work and you're a programmer, say you're a mail sorter down at the Post Office. They're not going to ask you about the latest Elvis stamp.

3.) ROTATE USERNAMES/NICS

The desire for convenience often gets people in trouble. They use the same usernames on multiple sites/forums. That's fine for the daytime, open web. Not so much for the darknet. It breaks anonymity. Take forums for example. When your username becomes infamous for a wealth of knowledge, change it. Create a new one. Don't tell anyone. Entropy rises when many users swap information like this on a frequent basis. Maintain separate personas: one for the darknet, one for regular internet. Memorization is better than writing it down.

4.) NEVER TURN **off your router**

I never turn mine off. Ever. If it is constantly going on and off while Freenet, Tor, I2P or IRC is running, after a while clues will surface as to who I really am, provided a sufficiently determined adversary has the resources to do it (NSA). The cost in power is negligible, so don't go cheap with anonymity. As the saying goes: out of speed, anonymity and reliability, you can only pick two, but make up for the lost component by acting *smart*.

5.) POWER IN NUMBERS: **Bandwidth**

Don't be stingy with your connection. The more you participate in the storm of users (Freenet, I2P), the more cloaked you will be. It is better to run 24/7 if you can. This makes it more difficult for an adversary to discern if you sent a file to someone else, or if you are merely the middle man to some file sent by a total unknown on the other side of the globe. Besides this, leaving the program running just makes it a lot faster network in general for other users. Think *Safety in Numbers*.

6.) OPTIONAL (**but smart**)

In the browser settings, set browser.safebrowsing.enabled and browser.safebrowsing.malware.enabled to false. Search goliaths like Google and Microsoft do not need to know the website URLs you visit.

Get into the habit of flushing the cache--cookies, etc. You can set this to do it automatically upon exit of the browser.

Refrain from using Foxy Proxy to selective proxy .i2p links. You don't want to be sent to the clearnet. If an I2P website is a honeypot, your Firefox browser can send a unique identifier in the referrer, in which case... anonymity broken.

At this point you're probably thinking this is way more headaches than it is worth. And you'd be right...in the beginning. But anything worth doing is usually hard at the outset. I as well as my colleagues do all of these things only because we have done them for years.

We do them every day.

Are we thinking about them?

No, not in the least on account of smart habits done daily. Do you think intently about starting your car? Pulling out of the driveway? No. But it's a good bet you were petrified to do it when you were sixteen. And pulling out of your driveway is a very complex action, as are the aforementioned suggestions. Just one of your brain cells is more complex than a 747. Don't waste any of them.

Torrents and Eepsites

FIRST THINGS FIRST. Install not only the NoScript plugin, but also the Cookie Whitelist (Buttons). Ideally you want to block everything when surfing Eepsites. There are a multitude of add-ons on the

Firefox site but you do not need all of them. You only need the ones that preserve your anonymity.

INSTALL QUICKPROXY, also at the Firefox site. Restart. Then open the proxy settings using the edit tab and then browse to "Preferences" and "Advanced". Then "Settings". Change your proxy settings to:

127.0.0.1 for HTTP Proxy, Port 4444 and 127.0.0.1 and port 4445 for SSL Proxy. Ensure Socks v4 is checked.

CLICK "OKAY" and exit out. If you've configured it correctly you should be able to click the QuickProxy icon (lower corner of browser) when you browse Eepsites. You can also paste in .i2p websites and hit "Go" the old fashioned way.

Torrents

AN OPTION for torrents is to use I2PSnark. If you're a beginner, ensure the service is running by opening a terminal and inputing:

```
$ I2PROUTER STATUS
```

IF IT IS NOT RUNNING, start it with:

```
$ I2PROUTER STATUS
```

THEN BROWSE via Firefox to

HTTP://LOCALHOST:7657/I2PSNARK/

AT THE MAIN I2PSNARK PAGE, you can see it running. Now you can create a torrent. Move a torrent and the data into

~/.I2P/I2PSNARK

THE OTHER OPTION is to paste the data you want to seed to the same directory, and in my case, this is usually PDFs and technical manuals. At the Tracker option, you can choose whatever method you wish or create an entirely new torrent. I2PSnark will create the new torrent and set it in a queue. All that remains to be done is to click Start in the top corner and away you go.

Get your torrents from Postman's tracker:

HTTP://TRACKER2.POSTMAN.I2P/

TORRENTS MIGHT BE slow at first, but do not get discouraged. You will have far faster downloads on I2P than you ever will Tor. One can never have enough good karma in this world.

FACEBOOK AND OTHER MISFITS

Facebook is a bit of a mixed bag where ethics is concerned. On the one hand, it is immensely popular and profit-inducing for a reason: people love to chat with relatives, old neighborhood friends, girlfriends, mistresses and political liaisons, all in real-time. People love connections. The feeling of unity and solidarity. The benefits are fairly immediate if you're the type of individual who likes instant gratification. There is nothing quite like the feeling of seeing old friends on your friend's list who you have not seen in twenty-five years, now instantly accessible for a chat session at just about any time of day.

It used to be that Facebook didn't rely as much on the IP address as a P2P network did. Times have changed. Nowadays, all of your personal information is theirs for the taking, and in some cases offered up on a digital platter by endusers. Your real name, phone number, who your past and present friends are, and even your pets are all valuable data as it can be targeted with advertising tailored to every atom of your personality. What could go wrong, you ask?

One problem facing Facebook users is that it is all too easy for Facebook to give this treasure trove of data up to the highest bidder.

Worse, Facebook acts not as a protector of the 4th amendment, but as an destroyer of it. Many government agencies and local law enforcement have relied on Facebook profiles to establish alibis, reveal private emails, and prove or disprove acts that may be criminal or not. Read the Facebook privacy policy for yourself:

"WE MAY ALSO SHARE information when we have a good faith belief it is necessary to prevent fraud or other illegal activity, to prevent imminent bodily harm, or to protect ourselves and you from people violating our Statement of Rights and Responsibilities. This may include sharing information with other companies, lawyers, courts or other government entities."

THEY'RE MANDATED by the government to abide by subpoenas for user information data except any private messages that are unopened and are less than 181 days of age (these require a warrant). The problem is that the Supreme Court never recognized a 4th amendment right to privacy. That is, data being shared with third parties, so the government pretty much has a blank check to engage in "shooting-fish-in-a-barrel" type expeditions for subscriber information that may or may not have anything to do with any criminal acts.

State and corporation are thus conjoined at the hip in a quasi-fascism that is difficult to defeat and predict, nevermind the fact that the government often, when it has nothing else to do, creates laws that are meant to be broken--over and over (speed limits, anyone?).

Thus, outside of discussions on anonymity, there is a not much to do when the enemy's archers are standing upon the castle towers with flaming arrows aimed at the exposed king. But we'll try nevertheless.

Be mindful of what you type on Facebook. Actually, be paranoid, unless you are one of the king's fools. This should go without saying, but the neverending stream of fools on Facebook often don't even recognize your need for privacy or anonymity to say nothing of their own. They get so accustomed to the personalized interface that you start to think they've got in it for you with their shouting your real name across the internet.

You are not anonymous here, or on any other social media site--Twitter, Pinterest, Google Plus, etc.

In fact, a new Facebook account has even less privacy than one on a P2P network like Emule. Where emule is concerned, you only had to worry about the ip address. With Facebook, your private life belongs to them unless you take drastic action to prevent it. Yes, you may have heard more than a few complaints from a few peasants about the lack of privacy on Social Media. It hasn't failed to reached the ears of the ivory tower executives at Facebook, Inc. But what do they really think of anonymity?

THE ANOMALY: **Anonymous Facebook Login**

IN APRIL OF 2014, CEO Mark Zuckerberg announced that Facebook planned to implement "Anonymous Login" for all users. It was a misnomer in the same way that "cat owner" is a misnomer. It offers more privacy, certainly, but not anonymity. It doesn't come close to anonymity since you cannot login to Facebook *anonymously*. What it means is that, using your Facebook login, you can sign in to other websites, say at Ars Technica or Wired, and make comments without having to grant access to the treasure of data Facebook holds on you: your list of contacts, relatives, friends, favorite cereals and the fact you hate cats with a brimstone passion.

Presently they are testing this so called "anonymity" service with a smattering of social sites and forums so as to better "benefit the end-user", as Zuckerberg claims--grant more control to its userbase on some of the data that gets transferred. Notice the word "some"... of the data. Not all.

And herein is the fallacy: most people, especially those on social media, do not know the difference between anonymity and privacy. Thus the masses will gobble it up. Certainly signing up for a new service can be cumbersome--email, check link, clink on link, fill out forms, click another link in email, fill out more forms. It's a breath of fresh air to know simpler times are in the pipeline, but let's call it what is: efficiency, not anonymity.

Most people will think Facebook will stand true to their anonymity statement, but the truth of it is that they lied to their userbase right out of the gate, trading the mundane term *privacy* for the much loftier goal of *anonymity*. Facebook knows all about these third party sites you visit, and is willing to offer the data up to the highest bidder.

Your behavior, your identity, your favorites, all are a win-win for Facebook, and a lose-lose for the third party sites and *you*. If a nosy judge wants to uncloak you on a third party site over some "slanderous" comment you made, they need not go to the third party site. They will go to Facebook. They know the name you signed in with, the time you made the comment, the IP address you used to bounce to the discussion. Checkmate.

In an interview with Wired's Steve Levy, Zuckerberg had this to say about their new vision:

"WHEN WE WERE A SMALLER COMPANY, Facebook login was widely adopted, and the growth rate for it has been quite quick. But in order to get to the next level and become more ubiquitous, it needs to be trusted even more. We're a bigger company now and people have more questions. We need to give people more control over their information so that everyone feels comfortable using these products."

SOUNDS SUSPICIOUS, does it not? Well, that's not to say it's good for the goose either. In this case, the third party. Website developers who decide to use Facebook's API to expand their readership will have that decision come back to haunt them since Facebook "controls" the client that uses the API login. They can shut off the API for the developers just as Nevada can shut off water piping out to California. To counter this, they will be ever more vigilant in mining user data and be hesitant, if not fully opposed, to using this new "anonymous" setting as it grants Facebook absolute rule over its userbase. That is, if they were *smart*. Many are not.

HOW TO BE **Anonymous on Facebook**

FACEBOOK IS ALLERGIC TO ANONYMITY. You've probably heard that they frown on anonymous accounts. It is not entirely difficult to understand why. They can't target you with advertisements if they don't know who you are, and that's their bread and butter. From your behavior come the metrics, the things you buy, the places you enjoy visiting, your family links. From their own lips:

"WE REQUIRE everyone to provide their real names, so you always know who you're connecting with."

THIS IS a roadblock that fortunately can be overcome, since genuine names are not yet tied to any form of government ID schemes like driver's licenses or social security numbers (though they will be someday). And even then, the rules of supply and demand would dictate even this would not dissuade the need for full anonymity.

When you are neck-deep in the account creation process at Facebook, you need to enter as much false data as you can. The email address in particular needs to be created in complete anonymity. The big mistake most people make is assuming that clocking the IP address is a sufficient means to the end. However there are many tracking mechanisms--complex algorithms designed to match behavior patterns and preferential choices--that all the big social media giants employ. Just one slip up, a broken link in the chain such as connecting to a website that knows your real identity (BBC, for instance) can destroy your every effort. Before you know it, all the others have been alerted by bots, warning pings and moderators that you've talked to in that session. Endgame.

Ask yourself this: Would your closest friends refer to you by name if you attended a popular masquerade in New Orleans during Mardi Gras? You bet they would, masked or not, even if you had pleaded with them to protect your identity. Some of them might whisper your name, not really even thinking about their prior oath of secrecy.

Then before you know it, another who happens to have the ears of a fox overhears your name being called. In much the same way, Facebook identifies you by your acquaintances just as others might do at the masquerade. Who is he talking to? A woman? Young or old? Tall or short? Do they talk with their hands? Ah, that's Maria from Rome. It's really not too difficult, and neither is it for Facebook. Friends and family lists are hardline identifiers in Facebook and Google's algorithms. The facial recognition Facebook employs can only get more advanced as it scours the web for matches elsewhere: Flickr. Google. Amazon. Twitter. Mugshot sites. Surveillance videos. Then there are photos of you to worry about: photos your friends have that are out of your control.

Facebook installs super cookies on your machine (or one of their many 3rd party enforcers) that tracks you in a number of ways: by Sid number, MAC address, etc. It continues to track you even after you've logged out of all your social media sites. There can be no such event as 100% anonymity just as there can be no such thing as a perfect human. We are the weak links.

But fear not, young Jedi. All is not yet lost.

While true anonymity is difficult, it is not impossible. We can approach 98% anonymity with some smart decisions. First things first. Invest in a VPN account. The more walls we have between us and the target, the stronger the cloak. Visibility is cloudy in a VPN as they shield many of your moves. Location awareness is difficult to detect using a VPN, but avoid free public proxies as Facebook and every other site has been spammed to death with them and have shielded themselves from those range of IP addresses. Thus, a proper (well-respected) VPN is the way to go. You will want speed to blend in with other non-anonymous users. Every metric counts.

You will need to disable most cookies from third-parties but allow Facebook for each session. Using Firefox portable, you can set the browser to auto-clear them upon exiting each session.

Set up your false data. Everything must be different from anything you've set at any other forum. Ars Technica, Wired, WSJ-- they're all in bed with Facebook to one degree or another. Ensure complete uniqueness, and under no circumstances give them your mobile phone number, as this will nuke your anonymity before it gets off the ground. That number, along with the IP, is used primarily for targeted advertising as well as by law enforcement. You may have noticed that Yahoo now requires it for new accounts. The reason is that it makes things easier to identify you.

Avoid a large group of friends and NO RELATIVES. This can't be stressed enough. Relatives, especially the elderly, love to gossip and spill details about the retched veal you cooked last night, or the cat you sprayed with the garden hose last week. What you don't hear in other's chat boxes at Facebook can harm you. Politely tell (never ask) others not to tag you or refer to any events that may compromise you: pictures, videos, music that your "real self" enjoys. Three breadcrumbs is enough to raise the eyebrow of the algorithm. Insist on them calling you by a nickname. If they refuse, remove them.

Never use the same browser for your VPN that you use for non-VPN sessions. Install Firefox portable in its own directory with its own shortcut and configured to the VPN BEFORE creating the

Facebook account. Never mix them up. You don't want cross-cookie contamination.

Be cautious on other social sites as well: Google, Twitter, Pinterest, MySpace. Facebook will not invest in the resources to find you unless you hand them crumbs of data yourself, which can easily be done on other sites you are careless with. So avoid being too specific about things related to your hardwired beliefs on those other sites, too: Religion. Politics. Ethics. Switch them up. Be a Buddhist for a session or two. Or a non-practicing non-denominationalist. Just be mindful of stirring up a hornet's nest. A friend in Thailand (an American) who was well known in Freenet insulted the Thai king on Facebook, prompting them to take a magnifying glass to his account. The end result? Facebook changed his name without his authorization--to reflect his *real identity*. Embarrassing. He'd posted a link to his page on Freenet as well and as you can imagine, his entire identity was uncovered by this loud behavior.

It is not possible to convert your existing Facebook profile into an anonymous one no matter how many tweaks you make. Changing the name will do nothing. The algorithm (think of the sentinels from The Matrix) will still have records of your online behavior as well as your IP address. Privacy, however, *is* obtainable, in case you wish to shield your identity from nosy coworkers or other misfits. In this case you need to change your username, that part of the profile others see then tweak the privacy settings accordingly with how invisible you wish to be. It is a bit of a double-edged sword since this will make it harder for others to see you--those you may *wish* to see you. You'll have to seek them out yourself and add them. And this, too, can reveal your true identity. Nothing typed into Facebook is ever truly invisible from the bots at their disposal.

TAILS

Edward Snowden. The name rings a bell for most people around the globe. In tech circles he is a visionary. As for the non-techies, a few labels come to mind: Whistleblower. Hero. Traitor. Regardless of what you pin him with, one thing is certain: He hates censorship and loves anonymity, the kind of anonymity that calls for untrackable execution. Before discussing anything, he insisted liaisons use not only PGP (pretty good privacy) but the end-all-be-all of anonymity tools:
    Tails
    It is a simple tool that frustrates even those in the upper echelon of the NSA. And for good reason, since even they do not know the wizard who designed it.
    Where Tor is the worm of the anonymous fisherman, Tails is the fishing box. The fish at the other end have no idea who is inside the boat, watching, listening. It's a hacker's tool but also a patriot weapon. Using it is a breeze: install it on a USB stick, CD, whatever, boot from said stick and find yourself cloaked and shielded from the NSA, provided that you don't out yourself. And if you're using Tails, you're smarter than that anyway.

Built upon the shell of Linux, it acts as an operating system and comes with an assortment of nukes to launch under Big Brother's nose: Tor browser, chat client, email, office suite and image/sound editor, among others.

Snowden preferred Tails on account of its no-write rule: no direct data writing. A breach from a remote adversary? Not going to happen. Forensics investigation? Nope. No trace is going to be left on the DVD/USB. Obviously this is a no brainer to use if you're an NSA employee looking to spill the beans on unconstitutional spying, as well as a must-have for political dissidents and journalists. It is armored with plausible deniability, the same as Truecrypt.

Tor runs like warm butter when you boot with Tails. There's not much of a learning curve, and no excessive tweaking required. You can use it in the same PC you use at work. Boot from USB or DVD. Do your thing then reboot back into your normal PC with no record or footprint of your Tailing. For all intents, you're a ghost on the internet. And speaking of ghosts, the creators of Tails are anonymous themselves. No one knows their identities. But what we do know is that they will not bow to governments trying to muscle a backdoor into the code.

Linus Torvalds, creator of Linux, said in 2013, "The NSA has been pressuring free software projects and developers in various ways," implying that they had made the effort, and all with taxpayer funds. A bit like the cat saying to the mouse, "Transparency is good for you. Sleep out in the open and not the damp and dark, flea-infested mousehole." They don't like secrets.

You might be asking, how do we *know* that Tails does not already *have* a backdoor? How do we know that the NSA has not already greased their hands? The evidence is twofold: the code is open-source (anyone can audit it), and the mere fact that the NSA made an effort to sideline end-users says they fear such a powerful package. They cannot peer inside to see what the mice are doing. Snowden claimed that the NSA, while he was with them, was a major thorn in the side of that organization.

At the time of Tails conception five years ago, the interest had already started to build up in the Tor community for a more cohesive toolbox. "At that time some of us were already Tor enthusiasts and had been involved in free software communities for years," they said. "But we felt that something was missing to the panorama: a toolbox that would bring all the essential privacy enhancing technologies together and made them ready to use and accessible to a larger public."

PGP is also included in package. You owe it to yourself and peace of mind to learn it. Spend a Sunday with it and you'll be a competent user. Spend a week and you'll be an enthusiast.

As well, KeePassX can be useful if you want to store different info (usernames, pass phrases, sites, comments) into one database. These two are like a good set of gauntlets no aspiring black knight would do without. And don't think the blacksmiths have just smelted down some cheap metal, either. The designers have gone to a lot of trouble to modify the privacy and security settings. The more they do, the less you have to.

This is not to say you should use Tails every day. Only use it in those times you feel anonymity is warranted. As mentioned before, if you start mixing up services, operating systems and mac addresses, you may blow your cover. Though Tails is packaged with programs that one wouldn't normally associate with anonymity (GIMP, OpenOffice, Audacity, etc) you don't want to leak info where an adversary might build a profile on you. You'd be shocked at how many applications these days "dial home" without your knowledge (hint: almost all of them).

But the true Achilles heel is the *metadata*. Tails is really lousy at hiding it. It doesn't try to. It doesn't clear any of it nor does it encrypt the headers of your encrypted emails. Are you an ebook author? Be careful about PDFs and .mobi files, as depending on which software you use, it can store the author's name and creation date of your work. But this is not really the fault of Tails. Rather, it is the wishes of the development team to stay compatible with the SMTP protocol.

The other problem with metadata is pictures: JPEGs, TIFF, BITMAPS and so on, which again, depending on the software, can store EXIF data--data that stores the date the picture was taken as well as the GPS coordinates of the image. Newer cameras and mobile phones like Samsung Galaxy are notorious for this, and even keep a thumbnail of the EXIF data intact for nose parkers with nothing to do all day but to sniff through other people's property. A fake GPS spoofer may be useful but even that won't eliminate the exif data. You'll need a separate app for this. You might even go so far as to only use formats that don't store any metadata at all. Plain-text is one option, though even that can be watermarked.

You might think, "Can I hide Tails activity?" The short answer is: maybe. It depends on the resources of the adversary. And just who is the adversary? The government? The private detective? The employer? The fingerprint Tails leaves is far less visible than what Tor leaves. And yes, it is possible for an administrator to see you are using Tor, as well as your ISP. They cannot tell what you're doing on Tor, mind you, but there are Tor Browser Bundle users, and Tails users. It all comes down to the sites you visit.

We've seen how they can build a profile on you from your resolution, window metrics, addons and extensions and time zones and fonts, but to alleviate this the Tails developers have tried to make everyone look the same, as if they were all wearing white Stormtrooper armor. Some fall through the cracks, making themselves easier for a correlation attack by installing too many addons and thus marking themselves in the herd: A purple-colored stormtrooper, if you will. Such and such user has a nice font enhancer while no other user does. This alone does not break anonymity, but with a hundred other factors and sufficient resources, it might be the one detail that breaks the house of cards. Death by a thousand stings.

You might find Tor bridges (alternative entry points on Tor) to be a good investment in reading, as they can better hide you from your ISP. In fact, using a bridge makes it considerably harder for your ISP to even know you are using Tor. If you decide this route (and you should if merely using Tor can get you arrested-- a case in which you should NOT use the default Tor configuration), the bridge address must be known.

Be mindful of the fact that a few bridges can be obtained on the Tor website. If you know about it, others do too--even adversaries like the NSA, but it is still stronger for anonymity purposes than the default Tor config. Like Freenet, it would be optimal if you personally know someone in a country outside the USA who runs a private obfuscated bridge that has the option *PublishServerDescriptor o*. As always, luck favors the prepared.

HOW TO DEFEAT THE NSA

It needs to be said: The time is nigh for the NSA to dissolve. If not dissolved, then at least broken up as Nazi Germany was after WWII. Yeah I hear your eyes rolling. Comparing the Nazis again? Please.

But mission creep, the expansion of a project beyond its original goals (often after initial successes) has reared its ugly head once again as the NSA, once known as "No Such Agency", has far surpassed its original purpose: to secure American communications while gathering intel on our enemies. Unfortunately, it seems *we* have become the enemy. We, the path of least resistance, so to speak.

Intelligence gathering is now such a high priority to the NSA that it has gone global at the expense of sovereign security. The Tailored Access Operations (TAO) directive makes this obvious. Install spyware/backdoors on the enemy's computers... well and good until Snowden revealed that they do the same to their own countrymen. It's called *bulk surveillance*. The more data they have, the louder they are on claiming victory over the usual boogeymen: Terrorists. Drug lords. (how long was it to catch Bin Laden?). Emails, calls, even video is collected without your consent. You could say it is a system ripe for abuse, if it were not already rotting from the inside out due to the

Patriot Act (section 215). The very notion that the NSA can shield itself from Congress and the taxpayers who foot the bill should appall most Americans.

So, what to do when the mother eagle turns on her chicks? Answer: Build your own nest. First things first, however. Understand that if you are a high value target like Bin Laden or a Mafia don, the NSA will hack your internet-connected computer or phone regardless. There's no getting around it. If you're thinking, "Well, I paid a hundred clams for Drivecrypt and Phonecrypt and so it is safe from those hucksters," there is some bad news for you to swallow, cowboy. It is far from safe.

Drivecrypt is commercial software and closed-source, and considering the free offerings out there (Truecrypt--open-source and *audited*), the best case would be that you're only paying for the name. Worst case? The NSA has a backdoor within the code, or at least knows of an exploit no one else knows about. You can thank the NSA's BULLRUN program, which attempts to "insert vulnerabilities into commercial encryption systems, IT systems, networks and endpoint communication devices."

In an ideal, pro-Constitution country, the security of the citizenry against foreign threats would be priority one. Instead, we are faced with a well-funded behemoth that considers the monitoring and data farming of *citizens* priority one. Again, think "least resistance". Hacked accounts from Blizzard to Kickstarter to Yahoo occur every month and the NSA seems helpless to stop it. Only the truth is a little different than they led us to believe.

They do have the means to stop it, as it turns out. But it would require a significant rerouting of resources so that citizens are protected and not monitored and assumed guilty of some obscure crime. Worse, the positions of authority and influence are unbalanced and skewed. Cyber Command should not be integrated with NSA priorities at all. Their priorities should be focused abroad, *like all other military operations*, and not focused on citizens like some Eye of Sauron that creates crime out of thin air.

Luckily, a few have leaked enough data from the NSA's coffers to mount a counteroffensive. One man cannot undo the damage they've done, but a nation can: the millions can overpower their overreach and send them back to their proper place.

How?

Knowledge is power. This hardly changes over time and for the NSA, the knowledge resides in the network itself. That's where the NSA loves to probe and plant their bugs. To this, they farm all the data. Everything. Then hire analysts to sort it all. They monitor phone calls, satellite messages and even listen to the oceanic cables running to and fro to our allies. They tap the waterfall at the source, high above, or beneath our feet if need be. Good intel, ripe for the sifting.

But what is good intel to them? Well, it's whatever sets off the most flags: the people involved, their countries, the language they use, their religion. It all gets prioritized based on profiles their algo agents categorize. The more red flags, the higher up the totem pole it goes... into a wellspring of *metadata*. It is easier to cherry pick targets by examining metadata than to study complete emails and conversations. It saves time. It saves money. Metadata to the NSA is like cocaine to a drug dealer. It's valuable stuff.

The Systems Intelligence Directorate does the data sifting and sorting in this case, and is given billions by Congress to optimize its operations every year. They are always updating and honing their capabilities. Testing what works and what doesn't. A security group exists for each directive handed down by the brass. They do nothing but look for ways to streamline each infiltration tactic. Make it all blood simple with the push of a button, a button that has global outreach.

NSA agents can infiltrate at will, but they especially love non-updated hardware like routers. When was the last time you updated your router encryption key? Right. The NSA knows this as well. They have a backdoor for many of them and entire teams devoted 24/7 to finding exploits for every brand of router and password encryption scheme. This is all accomplished by the TAO (Tailored Access Operations). Once inside your PC, they can easily install a custom-made keylogger that records your keystrokes and will send them quietly under the radar. Your anti-virus will not detect it. Once this is done, it doesn't matter how complex your password is. Thus, it is easy to see how valuable prevention is.

But how does one prevent such an intrusion from a well-funded entity? The answer is **encryption**. Encrypt your email. Your data. Your boot pass phrase. Most people will not bother with email. Some might bother with data. And fewer still will bother with encrypting the entire OS as it can take hours for a 2 TB hard drive.

A few strict security suggestions:

I) The NSA does not like Tor. It's expensive to track users. When a lot of money is asked of Congress, they start asking questions and demanding results. They don't want *anyone* asking questions. So use Tor. However, do not say anything in an email that you would not recover from if it was broadcasted on network TV. And do not access your normal email account or bank account using Tor. Can you see why?

II.) Invest in an offline netbook or laptop for mission critical data. Make encrypted backups: Blu-Ray, USB, SD. Never allow the data onto your internet PC unless in encrypted form: Truecrypt containers/PGP encrypted, etc. Only decrypt messages offline and away from the internet. Learn about SSL/IPsec. Many Usenet providers offer SSL for free but leave it off by default. Turn it on.

III.) Whenever possible, avoid commercial encryption packages. The proprietary software is almost never audited, unlike Truecrypt. What does that tell you when they are afraid of people looking at their code? They're hiding something from you. When an encryption program is open-source, it is more secure, not less, because others can verify its security and detect any back doors. Word spreads like wildfire when a backdoor is discovered, but not if the door is nailed shut from the other side.

IV.) Your screen lock does not have to be perfect. It won't keep out any government agents but it may keep out nosy wives and friends. If however the OS is not encrypted and your laptop is stolen, all your data is theirs for the taking. Use an open-source app like <u>Password Safe</u> to secure them all from prying eyes.

You're probably thinking, why do you need all of these tools for privacy? Shouldn't Truecrypt or SSL for your Usenet be enough? The short answer is: it depends. It depends on your own level of risk. What you can live with if all is lost. And your loss is the NSA's gain, through threats of lawsuits and coercions and unconstitutional spying. They've almost succeeded in turning the web into a vast Orwellian looking glass-- with themselves as the only keymasters. They can only succeed if good men do nothing.

Trust encryption like you trust ammunition. And like ammunition, it can be learned in a weekend. Mastery however takes some time and effort, but know that by itself, it will do nothing but allow tyranny to flourish unless used for its original purpose.

<u>Endgame</u>

Hopefully if you have read this far, then you are now aware of some of the dangers that await us in the future. Clearly, having an exposed IP address is only a drop in the ocean next to the coming power grab. Unfortunately, there are always going to be up and coming social networks and applications that try to go above and beyond the use of the IP address to monitor you. We have seen it happen with many personal applications over the years: Internet Explorer, Napster, Limewire, Myspace, Facebook and the like.

These make their profits by subverting your personal choices and then targeting you based on those choices, and when you get right down to it, the longer you put off protecting your individuality, the less choice you will have in the long run. However, you now have at least an effective arsenal of tools in which to minimize this subversion. If enough people take notice, it may stem or even reverse the tide of fascism coming over the hills.

More and more we are seeing a gradual erosion of privacy. Some employers reject applicants to entry level positions based on credit score. Some employers demand Facebook usernames and passwords before hire. Some fire employees for words on a Facebook post. In the end it is all about control and eroding individual choice. For there is no one in the universe more unique than you. You are worth more than all the stars combined, and they know it. And want to control it. And there is no such thing as controlling just a little bit of a star.

Stay safe, always.

TOR & THE DARK ART OF ANONYMITY

PREFACE

You want what you want.

Invisibility. Anonymity. Ghost protocol.

You've taken the red pill and have seen the truth, and you don't like it. I don't blame you. I didn't like it either. But what I thought I knew about Tor and other incognito tools was only a drop in the ocean next to what's really out there. Stuff you don't find on many tech forums. They're whispered in private, of course, and it's all been rather invisible to you unless you hang out in hacker forums or Usenet. That is, until now.

Which brings us to you and I, or rather what I can do for you. It's amazing what a guy can learn in a decade when he rolls his sleeves up and gets his hands dirty. Private hacker forums. Usenet. Freenet. I scoured them all for years and what I've learned isn't anywhere else on Amazon.

Equally amazing is what you can learn for a few dollars in a weekend's worth of reading. That's me, and soon to be *you*. Where you will be by Monday is where I am now, only without the years of mistakes. Mistakes I made using Freenet, Tails, PGP. You name it, I did it. And boy did I make big ones: mistakes you'll avoid because after you read this guide, you'll know more than 85% of the Tor users out there, and know more about anonymity than most Federal agents. Yes, even the so-called super hackers at the NSA.

If you don't come away satisfied, return it for a full refund.

But I know you won't. Because once you've taken the red pill, there ain't no going back. You can't unlearn what you've learned, unsee what you've seen, and you'll want more. Much, much more.

First off, we're not sticking with the basics here. If all you want is Tor for Dummies, look elsewhere. Where we're going is dangerous territory. It's shark territory when you get right down to it. But not to worry. We've got shark repellant and everything you need to surf safe. You'll reap benefits you've only dreamed of and by the time we're done, you'll have gained NSA-level anonymity skills with a counter-surveillance mindset that rivals anything Anonymous or those goons at the NSA can counter with.

Speaking of which, they won't have a clue as to how to find you.

Secondly, for a few dollars you will know every exploit those superhackers like to wield against Tor users and more: How to avoid NSA tracking. Bitcoin anonymity (*real* anonymity), opsec advice and Darknet markets and Darkcoins and, well, it's a long list frankly but by the time you're done you'll be a Darknet *artist* when it comes to marketplaces and buying things incognito.

Third, we'll go over many techniques used by the CIA and FBI to entrap users. False confessions. Clickbait. Tor honeypots. It's all the same. You'll learn the same techniques used to catch terrorists, hackers and the group Anonymous and couriers for Reloaded. Baits and Lures and how to spot an LEA agent from a mile away. I break it all down into simple steps that you can understand. A few dollars for this info will save you a lifetime of grief. No, you won't find it on Reddit or Ars Technica or Wired. If you're mulling this over, don't. You need this now, not when you're framed for something you didn't do.

Fourth... reading the dangerous material herein requires you take action.

The Feds take action. Identity thieves take action. Hackers take action. Will you? Make no mistake - This is not a mere guide. It is a *mindset*. It's professional level stuff meant to keep you and your family safe for a decade out, going far beyond apps and proxies. And it's all yours if you do two simple things: You read, then act. Simple. Because you know what they say: Knowledge is power.

No, strike that. Knowledge is *potential* power. *Your* power. But only if you act.

Fifth... I update this book every month. New browser exploit in the wild? I update it here. New technique for uncloaking Tor users? You'll read it here first. We all know how Truecrypt is Not Safe Anymore, but that's only the beginning.

Besides, freedom isn't free.

Lastly... The scene from Jurassic Park with Dennis Nedry, I believe, is a nice frightful analogy to what happens if you don't take your security seriously. We see poor Dennis try to get his jeep out of the muck in the middle of a tropical storm. Lightning unzips the sky and the rain pours. The thunder rolls. A dilophosaur bounds upon him, beautiful, yet painted across his ugly mug is a deadly curiosity as it sniffs the air and cocks it's head at Nedry - moments before spraying his chubby eyes with poison. Blinded, he staggers back to the safety of the jeep, wailing and gnashing teeth, only to discover a visual horror to his right: he's left the passenger-side door ajar - wide enough to let Mr. Curious in for a juicy evening meal - which it savors with a row of sharp teeth.

The point is this: Don't be Dennis Nedry. There are far bigger creatures who'd like nothing better than to split your life (and family) wide open if for no other reason than they can. Such is the nature of the elite.

Unless, of course, you tame them...

Not bloody likely.

ONE
IS TOR SAFE?

That seems to be the question alright. And to that, well, it really depends on whom you ask because there are always wolves in sheep's clothing out there who stand to gain from a man's ignorance. Many say no. A few will say yes, that it's 'safe enough'. The media, for all their expertise in things political and social, come up woefully lacking when something as complex as Tor is discussed and get a lot of things wrong.

Case in point. Gizmodo reported that in December, 2014, a group of hackers managed to compromise enough Tor relays to de-cloak Tor users. If you're just hearing this for the first time, part of what makes Tor anonymous is that it relays your data from one node to another. It was believed that if they compromised enough of them, then they could track individual users on the Tor network and reveal their real life identities. Kind of like how the agents in The Matrix find those who've been unplugged.

Anyway as luck would have it, it turned out to be kiddie script-hackers with too much time on their hands who simply wanted a new target to hack. Who knows why. Could be that they'd toyed with the

Playstation Network and Xbox users long enough and simply wanted a curious peak here and there. These were not superhackers.

But as is usually the case with the media, this attack attracted the attention of a few bloggers and tech journalists unsympathetic to Tor and frankly, ignorant of what really constitutes a threat. The Tor devs commented on it, too:

"This looks like a regular attempt at a Sybil attack: the attackers have signed up many new relays in hopes of becoming a large fraction of the network. But even though they are running thousands of new relays, their relays currently make up less than 1% of the Tor network by capacity. We are working now to remove these relays from the network before they become a threat, and we don't expect any anonymity or performance effects based on what we've seen so far."

What those conspiracy bloggers failed to report was that any decentralized network like Tor is a prime target for attacks such as the above. But to truly stand a chance at punching a hole through this matrix, hackers would need Tor to implicitly trust every new node that comes online. That doesn't happen.

It also takes time for fresh relays to gather traffic - some as long as sixty days or more and the *likelihood* of being reported is rather high since the IP addresses are out in the open - which only speeds up malicious reporting. The *real* danger, and has been since inception, is scaring Tor users to less secure methods of communication. That's what the NSA wants. The CIA already does this in foreign countries. Now the NSA is following their lead.

TWO
RISKS OF USING TOR

The REAL Risk of Using Tor

I LIST them here before we dive deep into enemy territory so you'll know what to avoid before installation, and maybe get an "a-ha!" moment in subsequent chapters. As you read, remember that having Javascript on is really only a drop in the ocean next to what is possible for an enemy to kill your anonymity.

Javascript

It's widely known that leaving Javascript on is bad for a Tor user. Ninety-five percent of us know this, but the mistakes of the 5% get blown out of proportion and thrown into the face of the rest of us. Worse, many websites now run so many scripts that it seems as though they hate Tor users.

One site required over a dozen. Without it, the page was/is/will be pretty much gimped. Sometimes not even *readable*. You can imagine what might happen if you were using Tor and decided to visit that site if it was set up to lure users into a honeypot.

I remember one researcher claimed that "81% of Tor users can be de-anonymised."

Bull.

That 81% figure came about because the targeted users knew little about the NoScript browser add-on, and likely mixed Tor usage with their daily open net usage, providing ample data for a correlation attack. But that was just the icing on the cake. They left personal details *everywhere* - using the same usernames and passes they do elsewhere on the open net. Bragging about their favorite Netflix movies. Talking about local events (Jazzfest in New Orleans!). The weather (Hurricane in the French Quarter!). You get the idea.

Volunteering as an Exit Node

ANOTHER DOOZY, though not quite the granddaddy of all risks, but still risky. On the plus side, you as a valiant believer in anonymity graciously provide bandwidth and an "exit pipe" to the rest of the Tor users (hopefully none of whom you know) so that they may pass their encrypted traffic through your node. Generous? Certainly. Wise? If you live in the States... hale no as my Uncle Frick in Texas used to say.

It isn't that it is illegal *per se* to do so. On the contrary, but what passes through your node can land you in hot water if you live in a police state. All exiting traffic from your node (i.e. *other people's traffic*) is tied to your IP address and as others have found, you put yourself at risk by what others on the other side of the planet do with your node.

Lots of new Tor users fire up BitTorrent configured for Tor and suck down all the bandwidth. It makes for a very miserable Tor experience for other users. You may get served with a copyright violation notice (or sued), or perhaps raided if child porn flows out of your pipes. Think carefully and do your research before taking on such a risky charge, lest your computer be seized and your reputation ruined.

Running an Exit Relay From Home

RUNNING it from home is even worse then using cloud storage, and is infinitely dangerous in the USA and UK. If the law for whatever reason has an interest in your Tor traffic, your PC might be seized, yes, but that's only the start. In the UK, there is no 5th amendment protection against self-incrimination. A crusty old judge can give you two years just for not forking over the encryption keys (which if they had, they would not have bothered raiding at 6AM).

Use a host instead that supports Tor. There is Sealandhosting.org, for one. They accept Bitcoins and do not require any personal info, only an email. They offer Socks, Dedicated Servers, Tor Hosting and VPS as well as Domains.

We'll get into the nitty details later, but these are the Rules I've set for myself:

- Refrain from routing normal traffic through it
- Never do anything illegal (more later as it's a grey area)
- Never put sensitive files on it (financial info, love notes, court docs)
- Be as transparent as possible that I'm running an exit

Intelligence Agencies

THEY'VE DECLARED war on Tor and its stealth capabilities, no doubt about it. And though they will fight tooth and nail to convince you it is for your own good, really what it all comes down to isn't so much national security as it is national control: Control over you in that they know not what you're doing on Tor, nor why.

They don't like that.

It's quite pompous of them to spend so much money and waste so much time chasing you simply because they don't like you or your actions not being easily identifiable.

As you probably know, it's more costly to go after a high-value target. But they do not know if you are a high-value target or merely low-hanging fruit. As we've seen in the case of bored Harvard students, anyone can get into serious trouble if they go into Tor blind as a bat.

Even Eric Holder has publicly pointed out that Tor users are labeled as "non-US persons" until identified as citizens. It's beyond pompous. It's criminal and unconstitutional. It sounds as if they view ALL Tor users as high-value targets.

And by the time you are identified as such, they have acquired enough power to strip you as well as millions of other citizens of their rights to privacy and protection under the Fourth Amendment of the Constitution.

They do this using two methods:

The Quantum and FoxAcid System

HERE IS the gist of it:
- Both systems depend on secret arrangements made with telcos
- Both involve lulling the user into a false sense of security
- Neither system can make changes to a LiveCD (Tails)
- Both can be defeated by adhering to consistent security habits.

Defeating this requires a mindset of diligence. DO NOT procrastinate. Decide ahead of time to avoid risky behavior. We'll get to them all. A good, security mindset takes time and effort and commitment to develop but should be nurtured from the very beginning, which is why the RISKS are placed up front, ahead of even the installation chapter. Things tend to drag in the middle of a book like this, and are often forgotten.

Speaking of risk, if you wonder what truly keeps me up at night, it's this: What do other nations tell high-level CEOs and Intelligence agencies (Hong Kong, for instance)?

If the only thing I can trust is my dusty old 486 in my attic with Ultima 7 still installed atop my 28.8k dialup modem, then it's safe to assume *every* commercial entity is jeopardized by the NSA. And if that's true, if the NSA has to jump hoops to spy on us, how easy is it to infiltrate American-owned systems *overseas with our data on those systems?*

To that, if no corporation can keep their private info under wraps, then eventually the endgame may evolve into a Skynet grid similar to the Soviet-era East/West block in which CEOs have to choose east or west. But that's like trying to decide whether you want to be eaten by a grizzly bear or a lion.

So then, you now know the real risks. The main ones, anyway.

Every one of these risks can be minimized or outright defeated using knowledge that is in this book. The sad part is that most readers will forget roughly 80% of what they read. Those who take action will retain that 80% because they are making what they've read a reality: Making brilliant chess-like countermoves when the NSA threatens your Queen. If you do not take action ,but merely sit there like a frog in a slowly boiling pot of water, not only will *you* perish but your future generations will as well. Alright then. Enough of the risks. Let's get to it.

THREE
A FOOLPROOF GUIDE

Or As Foolproof As We Can Get It

NOW LET'S answer *what Tor is* and *what it does* and *what it cannot do*. You've no doubt heard it is some kind of hacker's tool, and you'd be right, but only from the perspective that a powerful tool like Tor can be used for just about anything. In fact anything can be bought (except maybe voluptuous blondes in red dresses) anonymously... as long as you're *cautious* about it.

Before you knock Tor, remember that it is not about buying drugs or porn or exotic white tiger cubs. It's about anonymous communication and privacy - with the main function being to grant you anonymity by routing your browsing session from one Tor relay to another--masking your IP address such that websites cannot know your real location.

This allows you to:

- Access blocked websites (Facebook if you are in China)
- Access .onion sites that are unreachable via the open internet

- Threaten the president with a pie-to-the-face...and no Secret Service visit!

It does all of this by a process called **onion routing**.

Think of it as a multi-point-to-point proxy matrix. Unlike peer to peer applications like BitTorrent or eMule which expose your IP to everyone, Tor uses a series of intermediary nodes (and thus, IPs) that encrypt your data all along the network chain. At the endpoint, your data is decrypted by an exit node so that no one can pinpoint your location or tell which file came from which computer. Due to this anonymizing process, you are anonymous on account of the packed "onion layers" that hide your true IP address.

It is even possible to build a site such that only Tor users can access it. Also called "Onion Sites," though technically challenging, you don't need a Ph.D in computer science to build one. Or even a Bachelor's degree. These Onion sites are unaccessible by anyone using the regular web and regular, non-Tor Firefox.

We'll delve deeper into that later, as well as construct a fortress of doom that nothing can penetrate.

Installation

INSTALLING TOR IS DIRT SIMPLE. You can download it from the Tor website at:

https://www.torproject.org/download/download-easy.html.en

If your ISP blocks you from the Tor site, do this:

- Shoot an email to Tor. Tell them the situation. You can get an automated message sent back to you with the Tor installation package.
- Go to Google. Do a search for any cached websites, including Tor, that might have the install package to download. Many tech sites may just have it in the event of all-out nuclear war.
- Visit rt.torproject.org and ask them to mirror it.
- Get a friend to email you the Tor installation. Ask for Tails, too.

- VERIFY the signature if you obtain it elsewhere other than from the main Tor site, verify it even if your friend hand-delivers it. I've gotten viruses in the past from friend's sharing what they thought were "clean" apps.

Now then. Choose Windows, Linux or the Mac version and know that your default Firefox install will not be overwritten unless you want it to. Both use Firefox but Tor is a completely separate deal. You'll notice it has the same functions as Firefox: Tabs. Bookmarks. Search box. Menus. It's all here - except your favorite add-ons.

On that point, you might be tempted to install your favorites. Don't give in to that temptation. Multiple add-ons that do nothing for your anonymity might assist someone in locating you over Tor by what is known as "Browser fingerprinting."

NOW YOU'VE GOT some choices.

One is to volunteer your bandwidth, which makes it easier for other Tor users but comes with risk. More on that later but for now just know that every page you visit with the Tor Browser will be routed anonymously through the Tor network.

There is however an important detail you need to know concerning security, and that is that your Tor settings are merely reasonable *starting points*. They are not optimal. We're still at the infancy stage and quite frankly, optimal as Tor knows optimal is largely dependent on hardware (network, CPU, RAM, VM, VPN), and so each person's setup will be different.

FOUR
WHAT TOR CANNOT DO

Now for what Tor *cannot* do, or at least cannot do very well. In the future this may change so don't fall on your sword just yet.

1.) TOR CANNOT PROTECT you from attachments.

THIS IS NOT LIMITED to executables but anything that can be run by way of code. This means Flash videos as well as RealPlayer and Quicktime, if you still use it. Those babies can be configured to send your real IP address to an adversary. Not good. So never run any executable or app unless you trust the source. If at all possible, go *open-source*. This also goes for any encryption scheme which you MUST use if you're going to use Tor. It is NOT an option. Some say it is but that's like saying learning Thai is optional if you're going to live in Bangkok. You won't get far that way.

2.) TOR CANNOT RUN torrents well.

OLD NEWS, right? Thousands still do this. Better safe than sorry, they claim. The only problem is they are safe and *everyone else* is sorry. Tor cannot do P2P apps like Emule and Limewire without making everyone else's Tor experience miserable. It simply sucks down too much bandwidth. In addition to some exit nodes blocking such traffic by default, it's been proven that an IP address can be found by using torrents over Tor. eMule, too, uses UDP and since Tor supports TCP protocol, you can draw your own conclusions about what that does to your anonymity.

True, you may be spared a copyright lawsuit since the RIAA likely won't go through all that trouble in trying to get your IP, but please spare other Tor users the madness of 1998 modem speeds. A VPN is a much better choice.

3.) TOR CANNOT CLOAK your identity if you are tossing your real email around like Mardi Gras beads. If you give your true email on websites while using Tor, consider your anonymity compromised. Your virtual identity must never match up with your real-life identity. Ever. Those who ignore this rule get hacked, robbed, arrested, or mauled by capped gremlins. Much more on this later.

FIVE
TOR APPS & ANTI-FINGERPRINT TOOLS

The Best of the Best

A few applications make Tor less of a headache, but they are not particularly well suited for desktop users unless you're doing some kind of emulation. But with everyone using mobile these days, some of these have benefited me in ways I never thought possible. Be sure and read the comments in the Play Store since updates tend to break things.

Orbot: Proxy with Tor

IT IS a proxy app that runs similar to the desktop app and encrypts your net traffic and protects you from surveillance and fortifies you against traffic analysis. You can use Orbot with Twitter, DuckDuckGo or any app with a proxy feature. I've used this for a long time now and have gotten used to it. Perhaps it is time to try something else.

<u>Invisibox - Privacy Made Easy</u>

JUST PLUG the InvizBox into your existing router / modem. A new "InvizBox" wifi hotspot will appear. Connect to the new hotspot and follow the one time configuration set up and you're ready to go.

All devices that you connect to the InvizBox wifi will route their traffic over the Tor Network.

Text Secure

TEXTSECURE ENCRYPTS every message on your mobile phone and is simple to learn. Better still, in the event you leave your phone at Marble Slab (Marble Flab to the Mrs.), rest assured your privacy is safe due to encryption. It's also open-source. Far too many apps aren't, and thus cannot be peer-reviewed by, well, anyone, unlike some proprietary apps like those offered by SecurStar (i.e. Drivecrypt, Phonecrypt).

Red Phone

THIS APP SECURES every call with end-to-end encryption, allowing you privacy and peace of mind. It uses WiFi and offers neat upgrades if both callers have RedPhone installed.

It's not for everyone. Though it's not as expensive as say, Trust-Call, there are convenience issues like lengthy connection times and dropped calls (ever Skype someone from Manila?) so it's not going to be as quick and dirty as Jason Bourne does it.

But the pluses outweigh the minuses. I especially love the two-word passphrase as a security feature: If you fear Agent Boris is dead and has been killed by Agent Doris (who now has his phone), you can request she speak the second passphrase. Simple yet effective.

Google and Tor

WHAT DOES Google think of Tor? Quite honestly I suspect they try not to.

They probably don't *hate* it like the NSA does, but they know that if every Google user used Tor on a daily basis, much of their ad targeting system would, shall we say, begin firing *blanks*. Imagine if a thirteen year old boy received ads for Cialis, or an eighty-year old woman named Bertha began to see ads for Trojan coupons, or... well you get the idea.

They don't mind donating funds, either, since this allows a future stake in the technology (sort of). To that, they've not only donated to Tor, but to Freenet as well and even Mars rover technology. All kinds of crazy things. They never know which technology is going to rocket into orbit a week or year from now so they throw money around like Scrooge on Christmas morning.

Captchas

AT TIMES you'll be using Tor and find that Google spits this requirement out in order to prove you're human. This, on account of their massive analyses on search queries, is what drives some Tor users to think Google has it out for them.

However, Google has to put up with lots of spammers and general thievery; bots hammering the servers with tons of queries in short amounts of time that put undue strain on the servers can be one thing, but it can also happen if your employer uses proxies - many employees working for the same company that uses one of these can set off a red flag.

When your Tor circuit switches to a new one, usually it solves itself. There are other search engines like DuckDuckGo you can use, however.

You may find websites do the same thing. Again, this is on account of so many exit nodes (all of which are publicly visible to any website admin), slamming the website with traffic such that the hammering behavior resemble those of a bot, the kind Russian and Chinese outfits like to use.

SpiderOak

NORMALLY I WARN against using Cloud Service for anything you want private. SpiderOak one exception, with some reservation. It's a decent enough alternative to DropBox as it is coded with "Zero Knowledge" (so say the developer) and when you install it, a set of encryption keys is created client-side. When you upload data to SpiderOak servers, they're encrypted on *your* computer and *then* uploaded. Again, according to the developers.

They claim that even if a subpoena requires subscriber data, they could not deliver since only you have the keys. Not bad, but I still would not upload anything unencrypted. A container file, for instance.

The other downside is that it is centralized. Centralization means a single-point-of-failure. As well your data can be deleted by them at any time (true with any online service really). Remember that between you and a judge, they will always side with the judge.

SIX
TAILS

Ever heard of a "live system"? Neither had I until Tails burst on the scene. Tails allows you to use Tor and avoid tracking and censorship and in just about any location you could want. It houses its own operating system and is designed for those on the go.

You can run it via USB stick, SD or even a DVD. Pretty handy as this makes it resistant to viruses. It's also beneficial if you don't want your hard drive to leave remnants of your browsing session. The best part is that it's free and based on Linux *and* comes with chat client, email, office, and browser.

The downside to using a DVD is that you must burn it again each time you update Tails. Not very convenient. So let's install it to USB stick instead.

1.) Download the Tails installer at

https://tails.boum.org/install/win/usb/index.en.html

You must first install it somewhere, like a DVD, and then clone it the USB stick or SD card.

2.) Click Applications --> Tails --> Tails install to begin the installation.

3.) Choose Clone & Install to install to SD card or USB Memory Stick

4.) Plug in your device, then scan for the device in the Target-Device drop down menu. You'll get a warning about it overwriting anything on the device, blah-blah. Choose yes and confirm install.

Tails Limitations

NEITHER TAILS nor Tor encrypt your docs automatically. You must use GnuPG or LUKS for that (included), bearing in mind that some docs like Word or Atlantis may have your registration info within the document itself (In 2013, Amazon self-publishers discovered pen names could sometimes be revealed by looking at the code of the above apps and finding out the real identity of authors. Ouch.)

Personally I use fake info when "registering" any app I will use in conjunction with Tor or Tails.

OTHER NOTEWORTHY STUFF:
- Document metadata is not wiped with Tails
- Tails does not hide the fact you're using it from your ISP (unless you use Tor bridges). They cannot see what you're doing on Tor, true enough, but they know you're using it.
- Tails is blind to human error. Try not to use the same Tails session to begin two different projects. Use separate sessions. Isolating both identities in this way contributes to strong anonymity for your sessions.

Chrome

FIREFOX IS HARDLY the only way to slay a dragon. There's also Chrome. Yes, it's Google, and yes Google has strayed far from it's "Do

No Evil" motto, but like everything else in life, luck favors the prepared. You just have to have the right sword. The right armor. The right lockpicks. The preparations (reagents) are as follows:

I. INSTALL THE SCRIPTNO EXTENSION. It is to chrome what a mouse is for a PC, at least as far as precision aiming goes. It offers excellent control, too, even allowing you to fine-tune the browser in ways that NoScript for Firefox cannot. If you find it too difficult, ScriptSafe is another option. I've used both and came away very satisfied, though like everything else on the internet, YMMV.

II. FlashControl is a nice alternative to Firefox. In the event you don't see it in the Google Play Store, just search for "Flash Block" and it should come up (Google has a habit of removing apps that aren't updated every Thursday under a Full Moon).

III. Adblock. This one is just insanely good at repelling all kinds of malware.

IV. User-agent Switcher for Chrome. Install it. Never leave home (0.0.0.0) without it. It spoofs and mimics user-agent strings. You can set yours to look like Internet Explorer. This will fool a lot of malware payloads into thinking you really are browsing with IE and not Firefox or Chrome, thus firing blanks at you.

IT MIGHT HAVE SAVED Blake Benthall, 26 year old operator of Silk Road 2.0, from getting raided by the FBI (among a dozen other drug outfits). This was accomplished over the span of many months since they had to get control of many relays, and if you have *control of relays*, you can use sophisticated traffic analysis to study patterns in IP addresses and match behavior and browser settings with those addresses. Recall that any federal prosecutor will always try to tie an IP address to an actual person where felonies are concerned.

It bears repeating.

An IP address is considered an *identity* for the purposes of prosecution.

We're all a number to them, regardless. Those of you with student loans know this perhaps more than anyone else. This will change as time goes on of course as Tor competitors like Freenet and other apps evolve to offer what Tor cannot. Ivan Pustogarov said the FBI did their homework and when all was said and done, had more resources on identifying lazy users than a typical VPN would.

V. CANVASBLOCKER - *And* another great plugin for Firefox. This prevents sites from using Javascript <canvas> API to fingerprint users. You can block it on every site or be discriminant and block only a few sites. Up to you. The biggest thing for me is that it doesn't *break* websites. More info here but in case you can't be bothered, here's the gist:

The different block modes are:
</canvas></canvas></canvas>
- block readout API: All websites not on the white list or black list can use the <canvas> API to display something on the page, but the readout API is not allowed to return values to the website.
- fake readout API: Canvas Blocker's default setting, and my favorite! All websites not on the white list or black list can use the <canvas> API to display something on the page, but the readout API is forced to return a new random value each time it is called.
- ask for readout API permission: All websites not on the white list or black list can use the <canvas> API to display something on the page, but the user will be asked if the website should be allowed to use the readout API each time it is called.

- *block everything*: Ignore all lists and block the <canvas> API on all websites.

- *allow only white list*: Only websites in the white list are allowed to use the <canvas> API.

- *ask for permission*: If a website is not listed on the white list or black list, the user will be asked if the website should be allowed to use the <canvas> API each time it is called.

- *block only black list*: Block the <canvas> API only for websites on the black list.

- *allow everything*: Ignore all lists and allow the <canvas> API on all websites.

As you can see, it's powerful stuff.

Firefox Armor

BUT FIRST A LITTLE mention of something a lot of people get wrong. You might be tempted to enable "Check for counterfeit websites" in Firefox. Don't do this as it will relay sites you regularly visit to Google's servers. Google's "predictive text-search" is also bad as it relays keystrokes to Google as well. To change it you have to do it manually by going into about:config in the address bar. That said, let's look at some other privacy settings you might want to know about.

Javascript - Avoid like the plague. You may notice it is turned on by default under the Firefox options tab, though. By the Tor Developer Team:

We configure NoScript to allow JavaScript by default in Tor Browser because many websites will not work with JavaScript disabled. Most users would give up on Tor entirely if a website they want to use requires JavaScript, because they would not know how to allow a website to use JavaScript (or that enabling JavaScript might make a website work).

There's a tradeoff here. On the one hand, we should leave JavaScript enabled by default so websites work the way users expect. On the other hand, we should disable JavaScript by default to better protect against browser vulnerabilities (not just a theoretical concern!). But there's a third issue: websites can easily determine whether you have allowed JavaScript for them, and if you disable JavaScript by default but then allow a few websites to run scripts (the way most people use NoScript), then your choice of whitelisted websites acts as a sort of cookie that makes you recognizable (and distinguishable), thus harming your anonymity.

Ghostery and Ghostrank

NOT DEADLY, just useless on Tor since Tor disables tracking anyway. If you do use it, either could possibly alter your browser 'fingerprint', though not to the extent of breaking anonymity. Ghostery still blocks any tracking scripts regardless if you're on Tor or not. But use DuckDuckGo if you want to beef up your anonymity.

Adblock

THIS COULD ALSO CHANGE your fingerprint. Adblock plus has "acceptable ads" enabled by default, and there is also the scandals that Adblock has been in over the years, one implying that Google paid the Adblock CEO for Google Ads to be shown.

Besides, the basic idea of the Tor Browser Bundle is to use as few addons as possible. They figure that TorButton, NoScript, and HTTPS Everywhere is sufficient to preserve anonymity without the added risk of additional addons.

Whonix & Tor

IF YOU'RE paranoid that using Tor could get you into trouble (if you are hosting a Hidden Service), you might want to look into Whonix before running anything. Many power users who use Tor daily like the tighter security it offers. This is not to say that it is *better* than Tails by default. Both tools offer strengths and weaknesses meant for different purposes, and you may find one is better than the other for *your personal situation*.

Like Tails, Whonix is built with anonymity *and* security in mind. It's also based off of Debian/Linux, so it's a good synergy where anonymity is concerned. This synergy grants anonymity by routing everything through Tor. The advantages are that DNS leaks are next to impossible and malware cannot reveal your IP address. In fact, the only connections possible are routed through Tor via the Whonix-Gateway.

The question you may be wondering is: how much security is too much security? What's overkill and what isn't?

Well, you should ask how far will you fall if caught, and how much time are you willing to invest in reading to prevent it. Tails is easier to grasp, and if you do not expect attacks from sites you visit then by all means use Tails.

If you live in North Korea or China then there is a possibility of hard labor hammering worthless rocks if they see any Tor activity coming from your location that correlates to "things they don't like" activity... or anything else in the case of NK that offers hope. Guilty until proven innocent.

So if the above applies to you, use Whonix as it offers more security.

A few notable features of Whonix that make it more secure:
Anonymous Publishing/Anti-Censorship
Anonymous E-Mail w/Thunderbird or TorBirdy
Add proxy behind Tor (user -> Tor -> proxy)
Chat anonymously.
IP/DNS protocol leak protection.
Hide that you are using Tor
Hide the fact you are using Whonix

Mixmaster over Tor
Secure And Distributed Time Synchronization Mechanism
Security by Isolation
Send E-mail anonymously without registration
Torify any app
Torify Windows
Virtual Machine Images (VM)
VPN Support
Use Adobe Flash anonymously
Use Java/Javascript anonymously

THE FOLLOWING IS an example of a moderately secure system:

- Host Whonix on a memory stick with a flavor of Linux of your choice

- Use a VPN you trust (for privacy, not anonymity)

- Use Macchanger to spoof any mac address every session (Whonix does not hide your mac address from sites you visit!). If Macchanger isn't to your liking, give Technitium MAC Address Changer a try.

- Avoid regular calls of non-Tor WiFi tablets if using Cafe WiFi

- Know where every CCTV is located in the area you plan to use Tor

MAC Addresses

WE MENTIONED MAC ADDRESSES.

As technology would have it, your new WiFi/Ethernet card has something that can aid intelligence agencies in tracking you. It's a 48-bit identifier burned-in by the manufacturer. Sort of like an IMEI for your phone. If by chance you were not thinking clearly and bought your computer with Tor in mind using a credit card, you may later get targeted by an FBI "NIT" that swipes your MAC number. If that happens, you're toast.

The way to defeat this is to have a disposable MAC (the number, not the Apple product). One that you bought with cash with no security cams. That way you can get rid of it in a flash or swap it out.

They are also soft-configurable.

Believe it or not, Tails itself alters this randomly with every session. With a virtual machine, the FBI Nit may target a MAC number from the VirtualBox pool. Not really an issue unless they happen to raid your house and snag your system simultaneously. So swapping this out on a daily basis, as you've probably guessed, can be quite a pain. It's mainly for guys who run illegal markets. Guys who are *always* in the crosshairs of alphabet agencies.

But then, so can you. I've found it pays to think of oneself higher than what one is actually worth when traversing dark nets. Basically, thinking of yourself as a **high value target**. You'll subconsciously program yourself to research more, learn more, from everything from bad security mistakes to bad friendships to bad business practices. To that, you don't have to be in the top 5% of guys who've mastered network security. Being in the top 25% pool is more than enough to make The Man get frustrated enough to look for his flashy headlines elsewhere.

Whonix Bridges

IF YOU LIVE in a communist hellscape where even mentioning Tor can get you into trouble, using a Bridge with Whonix can be quite literally a life saver.

What Bridges Are

BRIDGES ARE obfuscation tools to cloak your Tor usage from a nosy ISP or government who might see you are using Tor, but not know what you are doing with it. To that end, Tor bridges are alternative ways to enter the Tor network. Some are private. Many are public. Some are listed on the Tor homepage. In a hostile environment you can see the value in using it to your advantage as it makes it *much more* difficult for an ISP to know you're using Tor.

What Bridges Are Not

WHILE NOT ESPECIALLY *UNRELIABLE*, they are certainly *less* reliable than regular Tor usage where performance goes. But the tradeoff may be in your best interest. Only you can decide if the performance hit is warranted. Here's how to do it in Whonix.

Bridges must be added manually since there is no auto-install method for Whonix, but it is not difficult. You simply must enter them into the proper directory:

/etc/tor/torrc.

IF YOU'RE USING a graphical Whonix-Gateway, then browse to:

Start Menu -> Applications -> Settings -> /etc/tor/torrc.examples

To edit your torrc file (necessary for bridge adding), browse to:

Start Menu -> Applications -> Settings -> /etc/tor/torrc

Then add whatever bridge you copied from the Tor bridges page (or a private one if you have it). Then restart Tor for it to take effect.

SEVEN
TOR AND VPNS

There is a lot of confusion among beginners when it comes to VPN companies. They read one thing and see something else in the media that contradicts that one thing. The cold, hard truth about VPN companies is that a few want your patronage so badly that they're likely to bury the fine print on their web page where it is difficult to read. Believe me, that's fine print that can get you sent to the Big House if you're not careful. It really is a minefield where these companies are concerned.

For this reason, you need to decide whether you want privacy or anonymity. They are different beasts that require different setups. And not every VPN user uses Tor and not every Tor user uses a VPN service, but it is advantageous to combine two powerful tools; one that affords privacy (the VPN) and one anonymity (Tor). Like I said, two different beasts.

But for what it's worth, if you like this combo then find a VPN that offers 128 bit encryption and that does not store **activity logs**. That's the first rule of business.

And here's the part where the fine print comes in. Many VPN companies *claim* they do not log a thing... but will gladly offer your subscriber data on a silver platter if a subpoena demands it. Between Big Money and Your Freedom, money always wins. They will not go to jail for you, ever. So do your due diligence and research.

Obviously a VPN service is not anonymous by default. Providers love to tout that it is, but let's face it there is nothing anonymous about using someone else's line if you left a money trail leading straight to your front door.

Enter Tor, slayer of gremlins and we-know-what-is-better-for-you nanny staters. Tor makes for an extra and formidable layer of security in that the thieves will have to go an extra step to steal something from you. Thieves come in all flavors, from simple jewel thieves to border guards who want to make you as miserable as they are. So it is a good idea to ensure all the holes in your Tor installation are updated.

Updated applications are resistant to malware attacks since it takes time to find exploitable holes in the code. But... if you do not update then it does not matter which VPN you use with Tor since your session may be compromised. Here is what you can do:

Option 1

Pay for a VPN anonymously

THIS MEANS NO CREDIT CARDS. No verified phone calls. No links to you or anyone you know. In fact, leave no money trail to your real name or city or livelihood at all and never connect to the VPN without Tor.

For optimal anonymity, connect to your VPN through Tor using Tails. Even if the VPN logs every session, if you *always* use Tor with Tails, it would take an extremely well-funded adversary to crack that security chain. Without logging, it's even more secure.

But always assume they log.

OPTION 2

Pay for a VPN using a credit card

CONNECTING with Tor when using a card with your name on it does nothing for anonymity. It's fine for privacy, but not for anonymity. This is good if you want to use Pandora in Canada for instance but not if you want to hire a contract killer to loosen Uncle Frick's lips a bit. Uncle Frick, who is 115 years of age and being tight-lipped on where the sunken treasure is.

Ahem, anyway, VPN services sometimes get a bad rap by anonymity enthusiasts, but signing up *anonymously* for a VPN has advantages. It strengthens the anonymity when using Tor, for one.

Even if the VPN keeps logs of every user, they will not know even with a court order the real identity of the user in question. Yet if you used Paypal, Bitcoin, credit cards or any other identifiable payment methods to subscribe to a VPN for the express purpose of using Tor, then anonymity is weakened since these leave a paper trail (Bitcoin by itself is not anonymous).

But the real down and dirty gutter downside is .onion sites. These are sites that can only be accessed by using Tor. The problem is that the last link of connectivity for these sites needs to be Tor, not the VPN. You'll understand what is involved once you connect with one which brings up our next question.

How Tor Friendly is the VPN?

THAT DEPENDS. Spammers use Tor. Hackers use Tor. Identity thieves use Tor. A few VPNs have reservations about letting users attain 100% anonymity by signing up anonymously. But if you signed up anonymously then you have little to fear since at that point it is *their* nose on the line.

There is one problem: the hardliners at the FBI do not like this attitude. In fact, they'd just as soon go after you if you use a VPN over Tor. Might a person come under twice the suspicion by using both? Maybe.

FROM FEE.ORG

"The investigative arm of the Department of Justice is attempting to short-circuit the legal checks of the Fourth Amendment by requesting a change in the Federal Rules of Criminal Procedure. These procedural rules dictate how law enforcement agencies must conduct criminal prosecutions, from investigation to trial. Any deviations from the rules can have serious consequences, including dismissal of a case. The specific rule the FBI is targeting outlines the terms for obtaining a search warrant.

IT'S CALLED Federal Rule 41(b), and the requested change would allow law enforcement to obtain a warrant to search electronic data without providing any specific details as long as the target computer location has been hidden through a technical tool like Tor or a virtual private network. It would also allow nonspecific search warrants where computers have been intentionally damaged (such as through botnets, but also through common malware and viruses) and are in five or more separate federal judicial districts. Furthermore, the provision would allow investigators to seize electronically stored information regardless of whether that information is stored inside or outside the court's jurisdiction.

The change may sound like a technical tweak, but it is a big leap from current procedure."

THE NSA DOES this without hindrance. We know this from Snowden's leaks that the FBI uses the NSA's metadata from private citizen's phone records. Thus, a VPN is not a truly formidable obstacle to them.

But this takes it to an entirely different level since if merely signing up for a VPN provides a basis for a legal search, then they can snoop on any ISP's server they want with no legal grounds at all to justify it. They've done similar things in Brazil.

But here in America, it usually goes down like this:

1.) Spy on JoBlo to see what he's up to.

2.) Make justification to seize PC/Raid/Data by reconstructing case

3.) Apply pressure to the right people with direct access to subscriber info

4.) Subpoena to decrypt subscriber's data. If they've done it once, they can do it a hundred more times. No Big Deal.

Solution

IF YOU'RE GOING to go the VPN route, then use PGP: Pretty Good Privacy. Never, ever transmit plain data over a VPN, not even one that offers SSL.

1.) Talking to police will never help you. Even in a raid situation. They wake you at gunpoint at 6AM and corral your family and threaten to take everyone to jail unless someone confesses. It's all lies, all the time by these agencies. A friend once remarked that a plainclothes officer once knocked on his door to ask him if he was using Tor, only to *make sure he wasn't doing anything illegal*. He answered yes, but nothing illegal sir. That gave incentive to go forward like a giant lawnmower right over his reputation. He was proven innocent later on but not before the cops dragged that man's reputation through the mud. No public apology came (Do they ever?).

2.) If they don't charge you for running a hidden service, walk out. In fact, if they don't charge you with *anything*... walk out. Every word out of your mouth will aid them, not you.

3.) You have no reason to justify anything done in your own home to them, or anywhere else. The responsibility to prove guilt is theirs, not yours.

But, if you are in a situation where you have to talk or give up your encrypted laptop, always *always* give up your laptop first. Laptops are cheap and easy to replace. Five years is not.

USING **Bitcoins to Signup Anonymously to a VPN Service**

BITCOINS ARE NOT DESIGNED for absolute anonymity, but neither are VPNs. They're designed for privacy. So why use them?

Well because any extra layer that strengthens your anonymity is a layer you want. But just as with any advanced tool, you can lessen anonymity if you are careless with it. Good, tight anonymity tools can be a bane or a boon: A boon provided you do your homework. If not, folly and embarrassment ensues, possibly a situation where, depending on the country you're in, you might as well slap the cuffs on yourself. It's sad that the times have come to this predicament.

So let's consider then how one pays for a VPN and obtains this level of absolute anonymity - recognizing that a VPN by itself will do nothing to further this goal. It is only one tool in a toolbox full of tools and Bitcoin is only one of them as well. You wouldn't try to repair a Camaro engine with only a wrench, would you?

Now then, back to Bitcoin.

Bitcoins are open source coins, a digital currency that utilizes P2P-like code, and like *real* money you can buy online products with it. Products like memory cards at Newegg or even a Usenet or VPN premium service. These are useful to us. Using these Bitcoins, you the end-user, completely bypass the need for a credit union or bank. Pretty neat. But, they're not without their shortcomings.

For now simply know that they are created from the collective CPU computations of a matrix of users (like you, for instance) who donate to their creation. Bitcoin mining is involved, and though you may have seen images of Bitcoins on websites stamped with a golden "B", they are actually not something you can carry around in your pocket.

Not in the way you think at least.

They have something in common with PGP - public and private keys - just like the PGP application, only instead of verifying your identity like PGP does, Bitcoins verify your *balance*. This is where **Bitcoin wallets** come in. Again, not a magic bullet but rather one tool at our disposal.

On that point, Bitcoin Wallets will only get better at strengthening anonymity in the coming years. They will accomplish this by breaking the trail to our real identities. Oh, and their development is constantly improving.

However as we mentioned earlier--embarrassment will result if you neglect to do your homework, for every purchase by a particular wallet can be traced. That's right. If you buy a new video card at Newegg with it, the same that holds your credit card details, and then subscribe to a Usenet service or VPN, guess what... you've now established a trail to your real identity. The FBI or Chinese government will not need baying bloodhounds to sniff you out.

But not if you make only one purchase per wallet.

This means never using it for *any* online entity in which you've purchased goods while your real IP is connected. It also means forgoing Google Plus, Facebook, Skype and all social media outlets with said wallet. Twitter, Wal-Mart, BestBuy and even small mom & pop stores with multi-social media buttons splattered all over their websites--these are enemies of anonymity whether they know it or not (more likely they don't). They are not our friends anymore than a grenade is your friend after pulling the pin.

A single individual might hold several addresses and make only two purchases a year, but if he cross-contaminates by mixing up (each transaction is recorded in the Bitcoin blockchain), then anonymity is weakened and in most cases, destroyed by his own making. Not good.

The trick is this: don't create a pattern. A string of purchases create a pattern; the exact sort of pattern Google and Amazon code into their algorithms to search and better target you with interest-based ads. Bad for anonymity and that's far from the worse that can happen.

We get around this problem by using **Bitcoin mixers**. These weaken the links between several different Bitcoin addresses since the history of that purchase is wiped by the exchange of Bitcoins among other Bitcoin users.

Bitcoin Wallets

IN ORDER TO subscribe to a VPN or buy anything online with Bitcoins, a Bitcoin wallet is required. More than one type is available to us. We'll go through each and list their pros and cons.

Desktop Wallet

This is what I use and for good reason: I have absolute control over it not to mention the thought of having to access my money on someone else's web server defeats the entire idea of anonymity. I would never store my encrypted files "in the cloud" and neither should you. At least, not without an insanely secure system.

Think about it. Would you bury your safe in the neighbor's yard with a For Sale sign out front? Same deal. The server could go down. The company could go bankrupt. Any person on the other end on the hosting side can install a keylogger without your knowledge. Nasty buggers, those things. Desktop wallets aren't perfect, mind you, but they are better than The Cloud. One downside is that you must backup your Bitcoin wallet, an especially imperative task if it contains a lot of money. I do this quite religiously every week, as should you. Apologies if this all sounds like a Sunday sermon, but some of this stuff really must be taken as gospel.

Mobility/Travel Wallet

AS THE NAME IMPLIES, you carry this on you to make purchases in the same way you would a credit card. Convenience x 1000.

There are many types of wallets such as Coinbase and Electrum but I found Multibit to be very easy to learn. It is available in both Linux and Windows and offers a pass phrase option. Even the balance sheet looks like a PGP interface, but yet is beginner friendly and open-source, so no backdoors. Good for anonymity.

MULTIBIT WINDOWS INSTALL

NOW WE COME to the instructions for a clean install of this work of wonder.

DOWNLOAD THE INSTALLER.

The possible problems we may run into: On Windows 7 64-bit which is the system of choice outside of Linux these days, it may be that the Java Virtual Machine (JVM) is not correctly located, or "Failed to create a selector" is shown in the error message. A solution is to change the compatibility setting:

Choose the compatibility dialog (right click--> icon - Properties --> Compatibility)

Choose: "Run this program in compatibility mode for Windows XP SP3."

Check the box: "Run this program as an administrator"

Multibit Linux Install

IF YOU'RE a Linux fan (and you should be if anonymity is something you strive for), then download the Linux / Unix installer here:
https://multibit.org/help/v0.5/help_installing.html

Open a terminal window and create an installer executable with:

CHMOD +X multibit-0.5.18-linux.jar

RUN THE INSTALLER: java -jar multibit-0.5.18-linux.jar

INSTALL.

THEREAFTER YOU WILL HAVE a shortcut to start MultiBit in your "Applications | Other" menu. If you see no MultiBit shortcut, you can run MultiBit manually by doing the following:

Open a terminal window and 'cd' to your installation directory
type java -jar multibit-exe.jar

NOW IT IS time to purchase Bitcoins. There are several options but what we want to do is execute an offline option; to buy Bitcoins *off the grid* which cannot be traced. Cash n' carry.

LocalBitcoins look promising as does TradeBitcoin. But as Trade looks down so let's go with LocalBitcoins.

- After you choose a Bitcoin outfit, you must signup for the site (anonymously) but be aware of the interest charges which vary from one to another depending on how much you want to deal in. For this transaction, use an email in which you anonymously signed up. That means:

- Tor Browser/Tails

- No Facebook or other Social Media/Search cookies present on machine

- Only accessed for Tor/Bitcoins.

CHOOSE 'PURCHASE' on the seller's page and the amount we wish to buy. Remember, we're not buying a house here, only a VPN to use with Tor. Once funds are transferred out of escrow, you will be notified.

Notice that the trader you are dealing with might be able to see your financial information, i.e. which bank you use, etc., but you can always opt to meet up in person if you want. This carries a whole other set of risks.

Check to make sure the funds are in your Bitcoin Wallet.

Paying for a VPN to Use with Tor

NOW IT IS time to pay for your VPN service... *anonymously*. Let's choose Air VPN at $9/mo and who also accepts Bitcoins for payment.

First: Sign up for the service but do not put any information that you've used on any other site such as usernames or passwords. Also, since we do not need to input any banking info, no money trail will be traced to us. The email we use is a throwaway email (you did use Tor to signup, right?)

Second: Give them the wallet address for our Bitcoin payment. Hit send.

Done!

Like any Usenet service, a VPN service will send confirmation to your email with details you need to use that service. Afterward you can see the details of this payment in your Bitcoin wallet.

As you can see, a Ph.D in Computer Science is not needed for this extra layer of anonymity. The problem with the mass of people on Tor, however, is that they cannot be bothered to do these simple extra steps. That's bad for them. Good for you. Those that wear extra armor are often the ones left standing after a long battle. But there is one topic left to discuss, and it's the most important:

EIGHT
REAL IDENTITIES OUTSIDE OF TOR

This is a big one.

One that I'm guilty of breaking because even anonymity nuts can crack under peer pressure every now and then and do something dumb like use Facebook over Tor (my early days, thankfully). A question I kept asking back then was this:

What kind of danger is there in using your real name online?

It depends.

Law enforcement and prospective employers who mine your social media presence for data are often worse than thieves who salivate when you announce on Twitter you'll be out of town for two weeks. Thieves, while unsavory and criminally deviant to be sure, rarely profess to be just. And thieves, as stated before, come in all shapes and sizes. If they take your private data without asking you first, that's stealing.

Employers can be the worst of the lot, as hypocritical as Harvey Two-Face, demanding transparency in *your* life but not their *own*. Make an inflamed political post or drink wine on vacation in Bora Bora with Filipinas twirling fire sticks and you could lose your job, or be *denied* one. Not kidding. Mention you use Tor and you may hear your interviewer ask:

"I noticed you're a big fan of Tor. Could you elaborate on why you need to use an anonymizing service? We like transparency in our employees."

Yes, I was actually asked this in an interview for a position that handled a lot of money. It came out of nowhere, but what really bothered me was the casual way it was asked, like every applicant should have something to hide if they desire anonymous communications. Maybe I was some rabid fan of Jason Bourne and up to no good. At any rate, they did not like my answer.

"Because I value freedom."

I came out of that interview perplexed, yet jobless, viewing privacy as somewhat of a double-edged sword since one *needs* an online presence for many higher paying employers. It did not sit well with me. I felt a little cheated to be honest and as I drove home, some of the mumblings I overheard later on became as loud as roaring trains in my ears:

Don't like someone on Facebook? You probably won't like working with them.

Like the competitor's products? Here's our three-year non-compete agreement for you to sign.

You use Tor? The only people that use that are terrorists, pedos and hitmen.

Soon thereafter, any time a prospective employer noticed "Tor" under the Hobbies section of my resume, it would always illicit a negative reaction. My breathing would become erratic as my heart raced, as if they were about to summon an unbadged "authority" to warn me of being *too private*.

He would dress a lot like Dilbert, only he'd be skinnier, and with a bumblebee-yellow pen and a clipboard. He'd have multiple facial tics and a quirky habit of raising a Vulcan eyebrow as if it were purely illogical to value privacy. I have no idea why he'd have a clipboard, but he always did.

My solution was to rightly divide my public and private identity in social settings and remove any trace of it on my resume. In fact, I did not give any indication on any social media site, either, that I was into any of the following:

- PGP
- Encryption, or encrypting files or Operating Systems
- Tor Relays
- I2P
- Freenet
- Anonymity in general
- *Anything* linking to Edward Snowden

Such is the nature of the masses. One simply cannot rely on Facebook or Twitter or Google to respect one's freedom to use Tor without announcing it to the whole world.

But with Tor, Google cannot mine your browsing session for ads. No ads = no soup for them. From NBC:

"The Internet search giant is changing its terms of service starting Nov. 11. Your reviews of restaurants, shops and products, as well as songs and other content bought on the Google Play store could show up in ads that are displayed to your friends, connections and the broader public when they search on Google. The company calls that feature "shared endorsements."

So I firewall everything I do. I use Ghostery for social sites and offer only pseudonymous details about myself. In fact, I try to avoid any correlation between Tor and any social media site just as one would a can of gasoline and a lighted match.

Anonymous Bullies

THE MEDIA along with Google and Facebook seems to think that if only everyone's name were known to them, then every bully from California to Florida would go up in smoke.

Vampirism, like bullying, comes in many forms, but if you've ever read Anne Rice then you know every clan is as different as diamonds are to lumps of coal. But they do usually share similar *beginnings*. Take adolescence for example.

Were you ever bullied in school? I was. I remember every buck toothed spiked-club wielding ogre who pelted me into nothing but a wet snowball in 7th grade, and it didn't stop there. How I wished it had, but not having Aladdin's lamp made things difficult. I watched as they spread like cancer, sludging upward to other grades for easier victims. Ninth on upward to 12th and even into the workforce. Bullies who'd make great orc chieftains if there were any openings, such was their cruelty and ire.

I recall one particularly nasty breed of ogre in 8th grade. He was the worst of the lot. A walking colossus who sweat when he ate as though he were being taken over by something in The Thing. Either that or Mordor. He certainly had the arms for it. When he arced an arm over me it sounded like a double-bladed axe slicing the air in half.

Harassment grew more fierce and fiery every year. Later I would learn that his entire family, perhaps his entire *generation*, grew up being the baddest of the bad - bullies that thrived on terrorizing to make a name for themselves. Every one of them went on to become cops in the New Orleans area. One died of diabetes. Another went on to join the ATF to fight the evil scourge called *drugs* (how'd that work out?).

I knew everything about these cretins and not just their names. I knew who their parents were. What they did for a living. Who they hung out with. What beers their dad's drank and with what porn mags. Gossip spread like wildfire in high school and no detail of identifying information was ever left out.

And yes, I told the principle, a great big lady named Beverly whose former job was working in some HR high-rise. I remember multiple times meeting her in that office where glitzy awards hung like a safari hunter's office and thinking if only she had an elephant gun I could borrow. Boom! My trouble's be over (so thought the 13 year old).

Meetings between my circus acrobat mother became fruitless and rather embarrassing. Absolutely nothing positive came of it. The point, however, isn't that nothing came of it, but that nothing came of it even as I knew **everything** about the scourge I faced daily. Knowing their identities did, well, not much of anything. Knowing their names did nothing. Knowing how many other kids they tormented did nothing and, let's face it, kids just aren't smart enough to band together and attack no matter how many times we watched Road Warrior.

We can see how bullying spreads on Facebook. Like anthrax. Little wolves ostracize a rejected member when a drop of fear is shown, so they crucify without knowing much of anything about him or why he's being targeted. Real names? Check. Real addresses? Yep. Everything is traceable now just as it was way back then. And still the orcs come in a blood-toothed frenzy like sharks to a wounded dolphin.

When 13 year olds begin hanging themselves in mom's bedroom to escape the torture, one thing is immediately obvious: what they really want is to *disappear*. They want *anonymity*.

But that's not something bullies think highly of. They won't allow it. Neither do they allow running away, not that a kid has the means anyway: No money. No car. No distant relatives in Alaska to run and live with and hunt moose all winter.

Anonymity is not an option. It's a requirement. It should be the law on some level but isn't. This is because if they gave us true anonymity, they would lose the precious power they wield over us. If Google and Facebook ever teamed up with the federal government to require ID to access the internet, we'd all be better off going face-to-face with an Alaskan grizzly.

Email Anonymity

THERE WAS a time when we didn't have to worry about what we said in emails. Security? That was something geeks did. Geeks and supergeeks who attended hacker conventions and scoured Usenet for zero-day exploits. It was the days of Altavista and Infoseek, when Google was still wet behind the ears and Microsoft was still struggling to satisfy every Dos user's whim. We wrote whatever we wanted and hit send with nary a worry about third parties intercepting it and using our own words against us. Sadly, no longer.

Advertising and search engines now tailor advertisements to individuals based on what you like and are sure to click. Trails are left. Messages are scanned. And Gmail is no different than Yahoo or Microsoft. In fact, judges wield more power with the pen than any CEO in any company in North America.

When a trailer is leaked or someone says something nasty about the government, you can bet IP addresses will be subpoenaed. Sometimes I imagine a lot of ex-Soviet officers are laughing at how many snitches the Internet produces on a yearly basis. Subversion to the extreme.

But is it possible to send a message that is *foolproof* against subpoenas?

There are, in fact, many flavors to choose from to accomplish this task. Below are a few rock-solid services. Combined with Tor, they grant you a virtual fortress. Anonymity squared if your message is encrypted.

The first is TorGuard.

TorGuard allows users to use PGP (Pretty Good Privacy) in email so you needn't worry about snooping. You get 10MB plus several layers of protection with mobility support.

SECOND IS W3, The Anonymous Remailer

Connectable with Tor, you only need an email address to send the message to (preferably encrypted with PGP--more on that in a moment).

Another is Guerrilla Mail. They allow users to create throwaway emails to be used at leisure. Emails sent are immediately wiped from the system after you hit Send. Well, within one hour at any rate.

ALL OF THESE services claims of anonymity would be pretty thin if we did not encrypt our messages-- which brings us to PGP.

PGP is the encryption standard of choice for many old users like myself, and for good reason. It has never been cracked by the NSA or FBI or any intelligence agency and likely won't until quantum computers become common. It works by way of key pairs, one which is public and one private (the one you will use to decrypt your messages with).

Worry not about the term "keys". It is not difficult to grasp and will be as easy as hitting send once you've done it a few times.

The first thing you must do is make your public key available. This is only used to verify your identity and is not the same as divulging your passphrase for say, a Drivecrypt container. Your recipient must also share with you their key so you can respond in turn.

The good news?

Only the two of you will be able to read each other's messages. The caveat is if the other person is compromised and you don't know about it. They will read everything you encrypt. Here is what you need to know:

1.) To begin, make two keys, one public--for everyone else but you--and one that you wouldn't even share with your own mother. You should back this key up in a secure medium, and remember that if it isn't backed up to three different types of media, it isn't backed up. If your truly paranoid, send one on an encrypted microSD to your parents in case of housefire. Yes, it does happen.

2.) IF HOWEVER YOU opt to tell mom, then she will need your public key (you did publish it on a public key server, right?) Then you can read it by way of your private key. She doesn't know this key (thank the gods!)

3.) YOU CAN "SIGN" any message you want over Tor or anywhere else (Freenet, for example, the highest security setting of which demands absolute trust of your friend's darknet connection) to verify it is really you sending it.

UNLESS NORMAN BATES does a shower scene on you and takes your keys. Your mom can then verify with your public key that it is really you.

4.) USERS you've messaged with (or not) can sign your public key as a way of verifying your identity. As you can see, the more people that do this, that is, *vouch for you*, the better.

Important

UNLESS YOU'VE GOT the photographic memory of Dustin Hoffman in Rainman, it's a good idea to store your public/private keys and passwords and also revocation-certificate to backup media so you can retrieve it five years down the line... should you need it. And believe me, you will!

Encrypt them in containers. Always print your key-file or pass phrase and deposit in a safe place. If you lose it, all documents encrypted with it are permanently lost. There are no back-doors and no way to decrypt without it. Also, consider making an expiration date at key-pair creation.

If you like nice and easy interfaces, try Mymail-Crypt for Google's Gmail. It is a plugin that allows users to use PGP-encrypted messages in a handy interface, though ensure your browser is air-tight secure and you trust it with your private key.

One More Thing

RATHER THAN HAVING to encrypt files and upload them somewhere unsafe, look at AxCrypt encryption tool. This is useful if you're used to uploading to Dropbox or Google Drive. Just remember that in the event you upload an encrypted file to "The Cloud," you will not know it if your password to said file has been compromised without setting strict security rules.

With that said, let's configure PGP for Windows

- Install Gpg4Win

- Next, create your key in Kleopatra and choose Export-Certificate-to-Server by right click so you can publish it to a keyserver. Get a trusted friend to "sign" and establish trust.

- Use Claws-Mail client that comes packaged with it or use Enigmail if you're using Thunderbird.

- Send a few messages back and forth to your trusted friend via PGP to get the hang of things.

- Optionally you can set a Yahoo/Gmail/Hotmail filter so as to forward any messages that contain "Begin PGP message" to a more private account.

Tor Instant Messaging Bundle

IT IS no secret that the NSA has Skype, Yahoo Chat and other instant message services in their hands, but as long as the Tor development team knows about it, they can do something about it.

Enter Tor Instant Messaging Bundle.

True anonymity is the goal of this application. It is built by the very same who developed the Tor browser bundle and like that application, will route all communication through Tor relays... encrypted *backwards and forwards* and hidden from the NSA's prying eyes.

There is also Torchat.

Torchat, like Yahoo's IM, offers encrypted chat and even file-sharing. Since it is built upon Tor, you are assured absolute privacy on what you say and to whom you say it. Both Windows and Mac versions are available and no install is necessary. Just unzip anywhere and run (preferably from an encrypted hard drive or USB-Drive) the blue earth symbol titled 'Torchat'.

A few more useful apps:

ChatSecure - ChatSecure is mainly used for encrypted messaging on mobility devices but they offer PC, Linux and Mac versions as well. From their website:

THE GUARDIAN PROJECT creates easy to use secure apps, open-source software libraries, and customized mobile devices that can be used around the world by any person looking to protect their communications and personal data from unjust intrusion, interception and monitoring.

Whether your are an average citizen looking to affirm your rights or an activist, journalist or humanitarian organization looking to safeguard your work in this age of perilous global communication, we can help address the threats you face.

TELEGRAM - THIS APP also focuses on messaging but with superior speed and is similar to SMS and allows for picture/video sending. There are also 'Secret Chats' that offer encrypted sessions. They claim no data is kept on their servers and you can even set the app to permanently delete all messages.

CryptoCat - Billed as an alternative to social media chat apps like those seen on Facebook, Twitter and the like, CryptoCat gives you encrypted communications using the AES encryption standard. All encrypted info is deleted after an hour of inactivity.

Freenet - This is the granddaddy of all anonymous systems the world over, both for file sharing or any kind of secret chats. Explaining everything it has to offer goes far beyond our Tor discussion as they are two different systems, but I include it here as an alternative if you find Tor lacking.

And it is not as simple as Tor, nor is it as fast unless you leave it running 24/7. It is not for everyone as there are all manner of criminal entities that use it and you will notice this if you load up any groups. It is hard to ignore and unlike Usenet, there is no one to file a complaint with. No one to report. It is anarchy multiplied many times over in many groups, but there are ways of mitigating the damage.

But for *absolute anonymity* and freedom of speech, there is no better tool to use if you have the patience to learn its darknet offerings.

FROM THE WEBSITE:

Freenet is free software which lets you anonymously share files, browse and publish "freesites" (web sites accessible only through Freenet) and chat on forums, without fear of censorship. Freenet is decentralised to make it less vulnerable to attack, and if used in "darknet" mode, where users only connect to their friends, is very difficult to detect.

Communications by Freenet nodes are encrypted and are routed through other nodes to make it extremely difficult to determine who is requesting the information and what its content is.

Users contribute to the network by giving bandwidth and a portion of their hard drive (called the "data store") for storing files. Files are automatically kept or deleted depending on how popular they are, with the least popular being discarded to make way for newer or more popular content. Files are encrypted, so generally the user cannot easily discover what is in his datastore, and hopefully can't be held accountable for it. Chat forums, websites, and search functionality, are all built on top of this distributed data store.

An important recent development, which very few other networks have, is the "darknet": By only connecting to people they trust, users can greatly reduce their vulnerability, and yet still connect to a global network through their friends' friends' friends and so on. This enables people to use Freenet even in places where Freenet may be illegal, makes it very difficult for governments to block it, and does not rely on tunneling to the "free world".

It is not as simple as using a Usenet provider's newsgroup reader. No sir, Freenet requires patience. Using Frost or Fuqid (Front End apps for the main Freenet program), it might be half an hour before you can "subscribe" to groups or download in the way you can Usenet. Some groups, like the Freenet group and other technical groups will be immediately available, but with few messages. Time will solve this. So keep it running in the closet and forget about it for a day or so if you plan on subscribing to a lot of groups.

It will be worth the wait.

Frost & Fuqid

THE TWO FREE front ends I recommend are: Frost and Fuqid.

Frost has seen a lot of improvements but I recommend you try Fuqid first as it is the first external app for Freenet that acts as as an insert/download manager for files. Fuqid stands for: Freenet Utility for Queued Inserts and Downloads and runs on Windows or Linux under wine.

The Fuqid freesite is on Freenet itself at:
USK@LESBxzEDERhGWQHl1t1av7CvZY9SZKGbCns-D7txqXoI,nPoCHuKvlbVzcrnz79TEd22E56IbKj-KHB-W8HHi9dM,AQACAAE/Fuqid/-1/

You will need to paste the above into Freenet's front control panel where it says "Key". It can take several minutes to load if you're new to the system.

After you've installed it, right click on the left side with your list of boards and choose "Add new board". For the name put in "fuqid-announce" with out the quotes. You will now find a new board called "fuqid-announce" in your list of boards.

Right click this board and choose "Configure selected board". This will bring up a new window. On that window click "Secure board" to change it from a public board. Now in the section that says "Public key" paste in the key below:

SSK@qoY-E5SKRu66pmKH64xa~R~w3hXmS5ZNtqnpE-GoCVww,HTVcdWChaaebfRAublHSxBSRaRFG91qCwsa3m-GF3-QE,AQACAAE

Now you have the announce board for Fuqid added to your Frost boards. The latest releases of Fuqid will be posted to this board along with the fuqid board on FMS. Questions? Direct them to the Frost or FMS board called <u>Fuqid</u>.

Passwords

GOOD, strong passwords are like having a couple of Rottweilers sleeping in your den. Most intruders will leave when the chaos starts. Weak passwords are like having a Golden Retriever. Nice and friendly and easy to trust around kids, but might just let out a little woof at 3AM when said intruder comes. Then he will hide under the coffee table (the dog, not the intruder).

I've heard for years that you should never use anything personal as your password. That includes family names. Favorite books. Movies. So what's the solution?

Remix your passwords with a symbol or two. If you think a hacker won't be able to guess the name of your girlfriend's locker combination, you'd be mistaken. It is dirt simple to guess even if you mix it up a bit. Computers devoted to this practice can guess many in less than a nanosecond.

BUT HOW DO you remember a password for a site used over Tor that has symbols?

Easy. Use a passphrase that is simple to recall for you only. First write out the first letter of each word, taking not of case and position. Insert symbols therein. For instance:

LAST SUNDAY, the wife bought me a Rolex watch and it was too ugly. Which when changed is:

LS,twbmarwaiw2u

The above pass is hard for a hacker to guess but easy for you to remember... assuming you are good at substitution.

Changing Your Passwords

PROVIDED you've followed the above to the letter, you shouldn't have to rotate out your passwords every 90 days. I'm sure you've heard from both sides of the aisle their say on the subject, but I believe research has proven that keeping a strong password (unless proof of compromise) is a safe bet.

THE RESEARCH PAPER FROM ACM/CCS 2010: "The Security of Modern Password Expiration: An Algorithmic Framework and Empirical Analysis" by Yinqian Zhang, Fabian Monrose and Michael Reiter came to the conclusion that changing passwords every few months did not, repeat, did NOT increase security:

at least 41% of passwords can be broken offline from previous passwords for the same accounts in a matter of seconds, and five online password guesses in expectation suffices to break 17% of accounts.

...our evidence suggests it may be appropriate to do away with password expiration altogether, perhaps as a concession while requiring users to invest the effort to select a significantly stronger password than they would otherwise (e.g., a much longer passphrase).

....

In the longer term, we believe our study supports the conclusion that simple password-based authentication should be abandoned outright.

Storing Passwords in Tor Browser

YOU MAY HAVE NOTICED that the "Remember Password" option in Tor Browser is not available, or so it seems. But if you look at the privacy setting and alter the history setting to "remember history" and "remember passwords for sites," it will no longer be greyed out.

Diceware

IF YOU MUST STORE PASSWORDS, a good option for a unique random one is Diceware - where you can get an expire date for any password months from the date of creation. You can copy any password to a text file then encrypt it and mail it to yourself or place on a removable (encrypted) drive or USB stick.

Remember: Tor does nothing to improve the security of your *system* to everyday attacks. It only improves security online, and even then only when used responsibly. Tor has no idea if your version of Windows is unpatched and infected with a zero-day malware payload that infected it with a keylogger.

One way in which a hacker could guess your complex password is if they linked your Tor usage with non-Tor usage and compromised your passwords from a non-Tor site. This is why you should never use the same usernames/passwords for Tor that you do for non-Tor activity.

PREVENTING **Non-Tor Activity From Being Linked with Tor Activity**

IT IS risky to browse different websites simultaneously and preserve anonymity since Tor might end up sending requests for each site over the same circuit, and the exit node may see the correlation.

It is better to browse one site at a time and thereafter, choose "New Identity" from the Tor button. Any previous circuits are not used for the new session.

Further, if you want to isolate two different apps (allow actions executed by one app to be isolated from actions of another), you can allow them to use the same SOCKS port but change the user/pass.

Another option is to set an "isolation flag" for the SOCKS port. The Tor manual has suggestions for this but it will lead to lower performance over Tor. Personally I like to use Whonix. Two instances, two VMs. One of them runs Tor and the other with Tor Firefox.

Keyloggers

YOU MIGHT WONDER what a keylogger has to do with Tor. Or for that matter, what a keylogger even is. You're not alone. In fact you'd be surprised how many people don't know and shocked how many techs consider them a non-issue.

In 2010 I caught up with an old childhood friend of mine I had not seen in over a decade. He was now an ATF agent. I was surprised and (falsely) assumed his extensive training meant he knew as much as an NSA agent when it came to computer security. Wrongo.

He replied to a post I made on a Facebook regarding the hacking group "Anonymous."

"What's a keylogger?" he asked. I waited for someone else to reply. No one did so I told him. He seemed amazed, dumbfounded, as though it were something only recently unleashed upon the net. I then told him that they had been around a long time.

But (sigh), there's a lot of confusion on what they do exactly. Some people call them spyware. Others say they're trojans. Still others, exploits. They're a little bit of everything to be honest.

They are *surveillance* software that tracks and records every click you make, every website visited, every keystroke typed. Chats, Skype, Emails. If you can type it, it can record it and all right under your very nose. It can even email what you type to a recipient on the other side of the world. CC numbers, passwords and Paypal login details are just the short list of targets it can acquire.

So how does one get in infected?

- Opening an email attachment
- Running an .exe file from a P2P network from an untrusted user
- Accessing an infected website with an outdated browser
- The NSA, if they can grease the right palms

Some employers use them to track productivity of employees. Some wives attach one via USB (Hardware version) to see who their hubbies are conversing with at night after bed. Parents use them on the kid's computer. So it isn't like they're 100% malicious *all the time*.

But they are devilishly difficult to detect. They wield an almost vampiric presence, but like vampires there are subtle signs you can glean without whipping out a wooden stake.

Vampire Signs

- SLUGGISH BROWSING SPEED

- Laggy mouse/pausing keystrokes in a text doc
- Letters don't match on display with what you type
- Errors on multiple webpages when loading heavy text/graphics

There are two types: software and hardware.

Software Keyloggers

THIS TYPE HIDES inside your operating system. They *lurrrve* Windows. Linux, not so much. The keylogger records keystrokes and sends them to a hacker or other mischief maker at set times provided the computer is online. Cloaked, most users will never see it working its dark art. Many popular anti-virus vendors have trouble identifying it because the definitions change so frequently.

Hardware Keyloggers

BOND MIGHT HAVE USED one of these. Being hardware, it is a physical extension that can plug into any USB on a PC and can be bought online by suspecting spouses or kids wanting access to their dad's porn stash. Keystrokes are logged to ram memory. No install needed.

Thus, unless you're the type to check your PC innards every day, you might not spot it until it's too late. They also can be built right into the keyboard. The FBI loves swapping the target's out with a carbon copy custom-built surveillance device. Granted, this is mainly for high-value targets like the Mafia but they're available to anyone.

Keylogger Prevention

- CHECK YOUR KEYBOARD for suspicious attachments. If you are an employee at X company and a new keyboard arrives at your desk one morning, exercise caution unless you trust your boss 200%.

- Use a Virtual Keyboard. No keystrokes = no logging!

- Use Guarded ID to prevent hackers from capturing your keystrokes. It works by scrambling everything you type, rendering any info useless to hackers.

- Use a decent firewall to stop a keylogger from delivering your data. A year ago, my Comodo firewall alerted me to suspicious network activity seemingly out of nowhere when I wasn't doing anything online. Turns out I had the Win64/Alureon trojan. I had to use Malwarebytes to detect and remove it. Norton was useless!

NINE
DARKNET MARKETS

Just how safe is a Darknet in light of the vulnerabilities discussed? The short answer is, *as safe as you make it.*

You are the weak link. The last link in the security chain. And although you need Tor to access Onion sites, the term can apply to any anonymous network - networks like I2P or Freenet or anything else that cloaks the source of data transmit, and by extension, your identity.

Which brings us to the *Darknet Marketplace.*

The complete list of such marketplaces on the deep web are numerous, and the risk of getting scammed is quite high. It's one reason why you may not have heard about them. They are often taken down quickly by either a venomous reputation or a law enforcement bust. Sometimes they piss off the wrong people and then spammers ddos the site. But there are numerous places one can go if you're curious about what is sold by whom.

When I say *sold*, what I mean is, anything you want that cannot be gained through the usual legal channels. And remember that what is legal in one country may be illegal in another. In Canada, lolicon comics are illegal and can get you in big trouble if you cross the border. But not in America. In the USA you can pretty much write any story you want. In Canada? TEXT stories involving minors are verboten.

The other difference is that there are safety nets in buying almost anything in a first world country on the open market. Think BestBuy. Mom and Pop stores. Florist shops. If customers get injured, what happens? Customers sue via the legal safety net and make a lot of lawyers a lot of money.

But the Darknet Marketplace laughs at any such safety nets. In fact, you're likely to get scammed at least a few times before finding a reputable dealer for whatever goods you seek. And it really doesn't matter what it is, either - Teleportation devices? Pets? Exotic trees? It's all the same that goes around. Whatever is in demand will attract unsavory types and not just on the buyer's end.

Therefore, research any darknet market with Tor, being careful to visit forums and check updated information to see if any sites have been flagged as suspicious or compromised. Some other advice:

- Always use PGP to communicate.

- Never store crypto-currency at any such marketplace.

- Assume a den of thieves unless proven otherwise by *them*. The responsibility is theirs just as it is offline, to prove they are an honest business. If you open your own, keep this in mind: customers owe you nothing. You can only betray them once.

Now for some examples of Phishers and Scammers and other Con men. By their fruits, ye shall know them.

1.) SILK ROAD 2.0 (E5WVYMNX6BX5EUVY...) Lots of scams with this one. Much like Facebook and Google emails, you can tell a fake sometimes by the address. Paste the first few letters into a shortcut next to the name. If it doesn't match, steer clear.

2.) **Green Notes Counter** (67yjqewxrd2ewbtp...)

They promised counterfeit money to their customers but refuse escrow. A dead giveaway.

3.) IPHONES FOR HALF OFF: (iphoneavzhwkqmap...)
Now here is a prime example of a scam. Any website which sells electronic gadgets on the deep web is ripe for scamming customers. Whereas in the Far East you will merely get counterfeit phones with cheap, Chinese made parts that break within a month, on the Deep Web they will simply take your money and say adios. Actually, they won't even bother saying that.

So then, how does one tell a scam?

Because many new darknet vendors will arise out of thin air, with rare products that will make customers swoon and send them money - without doing any research on their name or previous sales. A real hit and run operation. Hit quick and fast and dirty. Seduce as many as they can before the herd catches on to the wolf in disguise. Many are suckered, thinking "it's only a little money, but a little money from a lot of Tor users goes a long way in encouraging other scammers to set up shop.

When you ask them why they do not offer escrow, they say "We think it is unreliable/suspicious/unstable" amid other BS excuses. It is better to hold on to your small change than leave a trail to your treasure chest. And make no mistake some of these scammers are like bloodhounds where identity theft is concerned.

Do your research! Check forums and especially the dates of reviews they have. Do you notice patterns? Are good reviews scattered over a long period of time or is it rather all of a sudden--the way some Amazon affiliate marketers do with paid reviews that glow? Not many reviews from said customers?

If you've seen the movie "Heat," with Al Pacino and Robert de Niro, you know when it is time to Walk Away. In the middle of a nighttime heist, Niro goes outside for a smoke. He hears a distant cough. Somewhere. Now, this is middle of the night in an unpopulated part of the city that comes from across the street - a parking lot full of what he thought were empty trailers. Hmm, he thinks maybe this isn't such a great night for a hot score. Not so empty (it was a cop in a trailer full of other hotshot cops). He walks back into the bank and tells his partner to abort.

The other aspect is time. Some fake sites will set a short ship time and count on you not bothering to see the sale as finalized before you can whistle Dixie out of your ass. After finalization, you're screwed since the money is in their wallet before you can even mount a protest.

Fraud Prevention

ONE IS Google believe it or not, at
http://www.google.com/imghp.

Dating sites like Cherry Blossoms and Cupid sometimes use reverse image search to catch fakers and Nigerian scammers masquerading as poor lonely singles to deprive men of their coinage. If they can catch them, so can you. If the image belongs to some other legit site, chances are it is fake. Foto Forensics also does the same, and reports metadata so that it becomes even harder to get away with Photoshop trickery.

When it is Okay to FE (Finalize Early)

FE MEANS 'FINALIZE EARLY'. It's use online can usually be found in black marketplaces like Silk Road and Sheep's Marketplace. It simply means that money in escrow is released before you receive your product. Every customer I've ever spoken with advises against this unless you've had great experience with that business.

But... quite a few vendors are now making it a *standard practice* to pay funds up front before you have anything in your hands.

On more than one Marketplace forum, there's been heated exchange as to when this is proper. You might hear, "Is this guy legit?

What about this Chinese outfit over here? He seems shady," and others: "A friend said this guy is okay but then I got ripped off!". You get the idea.

Here is my experience on the matter.

1.) It is okay when you are content with not getting what you paid for. This may seem counterproductive, but think how many gamblers go into a Las Vegas casino and never ask themselves "How much can I afford to lose?"

The answer, sadly, is not many. Vegas was not built on the backs of losers. Some merchants do not like escrow at all. Some do. So don't spend more than you can afford to lose. Look at it the way a gambler looks at making money.

2.) It is okay when you are guaranteed shipment. There are FE scammers out there that will give you an angelic smile and lie right into your eyes as they swindle you. Do not depend solely on reviews. A guy on SR can be the best merchant this side of Tatooine and yet you will wake up one day and find yourself robbed. He's split with a million in BTC and you're left not even holding a bag. Most won't do this to you. But a few will.

When it is NOT Okay to FE

WHEN LOSING your funds will result in you being evicted or a relationship severed. Never borrow money from friends and especially not family unless you want said family to come after you with a double-bladed ax. If you get ripped off, you lose not only the cash but the respect and trustworthiness of your family. Word spreads. You don't pay your debts. What's that saying in Game of Thrones?

Right. A Lannister always pays his debts. So should you.

MultiSigna

SOUNDS LIKE SOMETHING from Battlestar Galactica to pass from ship to ship. A badge of honor perhaps some hotshot flyboy wears on his fighter jacket that bypassed a lot of red tape.

While not exactly mandatory, it makes for interesting reading, and is something Tor users might want to know about if they wish to make purchases anonymously. Here's what happens:

When a purchase is enacted, the seller deposits money (in this case, Bitcoins) in a multi-signature address. After this, the customer gets notification to make the transaction ($,€) to the seller's account.

Then after the seller relays to MultiSigna that the transaction was a success, MultiSigna creates a transaction from the multi-signature address that requires both buyer and seller so that it may be sent to the network. The buyer gets the Bitcoins and ends the sale. Confused yet? I was too at first. You'll get used to it.

Critical

MULTISIGNA ONLY EXISTS AS A VERIFIER/COSIGNER of the entire transaction. If there is disagreement between seller and buyer, **no exchange** occurs. Remember the scene in Wargames when two nuclear silo operators have to turn their keys simultaneously in order to launch? Yeah, that.

MultiSigna will of course favor one or the other, but not both if they cannot mutually agree. The upside is that is if the market or purchaser or vendor loses a key, two out of three is still available. A single key cannot spend the money in 2/3 MultiSig address.

Is it Safe? Is it Secret?

I don't recommend enacting a million dollar exchange for a yacht, or even a thousand dollar one as they both carry risk, but ultimately it is up to you. Just remember that trust is always an issue on darknets, and you're generally safer making several transfers with a seller/buyer who has a good history of payment. In other words, reputation as always, is everything.

Alas, there are a few trustworthy markets that have good histories of doing things properly, thank heavens.

Blackbank is one. Agora is another. Take a look at the Multi-Sig Escrow Onion page here with Tor:

http://u5z75duioy7kpwun.onion/wiki/index.php/Multi-Sig_Escrow

Security

WHAT THE EFFECT would be if a hacker gained entry to the server? What mischief might he make? What chaos could he brew if he can mimic running a withdrawal in the same manner that the server does?

If a hacker were to gain access and attempt to withdraw money, a single-signature would be applied and passed to the second sig signer for co-signature. Then the security protocol would kick in where these policies would be enforced:

1.) Rate limits: the rate of stolen funds slows

2.) Callbacks to the spender's server: Signing service verifies with the original spender that they initiated and intended to make the spend. The callback could go to a separated machine, which could only contain access to isolated approved withdrawal information.

3.) IP limiting: The signing service only signs transactions coming from a certain list of IPs, preventing the case where the hacker or insider stole the private key.

4.) Destination Whitelists: Certain very high security wallets can be set such that the signing service would only accept if the destination were previously known. The hacker would have to compromise both the original sending server as well as the signing service.

Let me repeat that MultiSigna are *never in possession* of your bitcoins. They use 2 of 3 signatures (seller, buyer & MultiSigma) to sign a transaction. Normal transactions are signed by the seller and then by the buyer.

PURCHASER STEPS FOR MULTISIG ESCROW

1.) Deposit your Bitcoins. Purchase ability is granted after 6 confirmations

2.) Make a private & public key (Brainwallet.org is a JavaScript Client-Side Bitcoin Address Generator)

3.) Buy item, input public-key & a refund BTC address

4.) Retrieve purchased item

5.) Input the private key and close

TEN

THE LONG ARM OF THE LAW

Can the law steal funds?
Assuming you mean U.S. law, no, since the wallet does not contain the money. The Bitcoin blockchain prevents this. Hackers cannot steal it either since two private-keys are required and they will have had to steal 2 out of 3 private key holders... not likely.

WHAT ABOUT SAFETY in using the private key?
Never irresponsibly use the private key from your Bitcoin wallet. Create a new one instead. Give it the same love you give your Truecrypt/DiskDecryptor master keys. Lots and lots of special love that no one else gets.

THIS SOUNDS AWFULLY RISKY. Won't I get caught?
Here is how most people get caught, and it really matters not what it is. Most dealers get busted making the usual mistakes:
- Bar Bragging

- Dropping too much personal data to strangers (I.e. Ross Ulbricht)
- Selling contraband to undercover law enforcement
- Snitches
- Committing crimes while under surveillance
- Managing an operation that grows by leaps and bounds (with loads of newbies making mistakes).

HOW FAR WILL the police go to catch you? That's a good question. The answer thought is pretty simple: As far as resources allow.

It'll probably be no worse than what Charleton Heston suffered being hogtied and dragged around the ape city, but know that some apes are worse than others.

It boils down to if what you're doing.

Case 1: In 2010, police in L.A. organized a phony sweepstakes scheme in order to lure in those with outstanding warrants. I kid you not, they did not come up with this idea themselves, but rather took it from The Simpsons.

They sent out close to a thousand fake letters under the name of a marketing group only to have a little over half a dozen show up at the La Mirada Inn for their free prize: A BMW 238. Nice, eh? Only the joke was on them as their smiles melted upon hearing those four dirty words, "You're all under arrest!"

The poor saps even brought ID to verify their identities. Dumb. They might as well have slapped on the cuffs themselves.

And this is an OFFLINE example. Imagine what one department can do by lying alone to an ISP or search engine. Threats of fines. Warrants. Bad publicity. Subpoenas of users. A bad reputation they are not likely to recover from soon. Police in Vegas in particular love to play dirty like this, dredging up old laws to ensure every member in that Ferbie operation has the book thrown at him.

IN 2013, a Secret Service Agent arrested several online by selling them fake IDs. The kicker?

They were all charged under the RICO Act of 1970. Originally created to put away mobsters, it allows them to lasso entire groups and charge each individual as if he committed the same crime everyone else in the group did... no matter the role.

Translation: The courier gets the same treatment as the ringleader, as do the buyers. Individually, not much prison time in the grand scheme of things in 1970, but being charged as a GROUP? Twenty years minimum. Al Capone never saw such a hefty sentence.

It simply doesn't matter to a prosecutor if you're OS is encrypted and they can't get the data. All they need to prove is that you were part of the *enterprise* operation. That can be done outside of your shiny new Western Digital hard drive by subpoena to your ISP and a few other services you subscribe to. They've done this (and succeeded) with the newsgroup porn bust years ago in which every member of that hideous pedo group had encryption coming out of their ears.

Here was the short list of rules in that group.

- Never reveal true identity to another member of the group
- Never communicate with a member of the group outside usenet
- Group membership remains strictly within the confines of the Internet
- No member can positively identify another
- Members do not reveal personally identifying information
- Primary communications newsgroup is migrated regularly
- If a member breaks a security rule/fails to encrypt a message=BAN
- Periodically reduce chance of law enforcement discovery on each newsgroup migration by:
    - Creating new PGP key pair, unlinking from previous messages
    - Each member creates a new nickname
    - Nickname theme selected by Yardbird (Group leader)

THE AFFIDAVITS READ like a Hell's Angels list of rules. And though I disagree with his (the website owner, not Yardbird) conclusion that "there are basically no nice people who provide case studies of OPSEC practices," I believe much can be learned by studying the habits of law-abiding citizen and criminal alike, especially considering the wide net over which the NSA is casting over *law abiding citizens*.

Remember that in Nazi Germany, if you slandered the SS, it was considered a capital offense. The film 'Sophie Scholl' is an excellent example of underground resistance movement for the right reason. It won accolades for its realistic portrayal of a college woman who stood up to the SS elite and was beheaded for it.

North Korea, Now. Same thing. They'd have little issues with doing worse. Beheading might be almost too lenient for them as they prefer prolonged, tortuous environments for their subjects. China? China has done some strange things, like outlawing stripping at funerals and banning Bitcoin transactions, and I do recall the violent protests by Muslims in 2010 and thinking "Those communist schmucks will round up all those screaming fools and shoot them at dawn and not look back!"

My Chinese girlfriend leaned over to me as we watched and mumbled, "They won't wait till dawn."

I like to think of Darkcoin as Bitcoin's smarter brother. Much smarter in fact, and darker. The best part of course being that it is constantly evolving.

Like Bitcoin they are a privacy-centric digital money based on the Bitcoin design. It's a design that allows for anonymity as you make day-to-day purchases on, well, just about anything so long as the digital store offers it.

With Bitcoin, anyone can see who made a purchase by only looking at the public blockchain. What Darkcoin does is anonymize your transaction *further* by using *Master nodes* - a decentralized network of servers that negate any requirement for third-parties: Parties that could scam you out of your coins.

Though few outlets use it, it is one of the quickest growing digital currencies out there, with an economy breaching over twenty million. Impressive. And that's not all. It's "Darksend" feature is quite fascinating--increasing privacy by compounding a typical transaction with *two* other users.

Needless to say, this is immensely attractive to a lot of Tor users who value high anonymity. Whistleblowers, journalists, underground political movements. That's the good list. The bad list though, well, you can never have the good without the bad: Terrorists. Contract killers. Tax evaders. Fallout players with the child-killing perk.

I hear the same arguments against its use that I heard with Freenet: Bad guys want to evade detection. Bad guys trade Darkcoins. You use Darkcoins. Therefore, you're a bad guy. Cue torches and pitchforks and black cats catapulted over the moat.

Heroin dealers love to use cash yet you never hear news outlets screaming about cash-only users linking to such a crime. Besides, the most corrupt money launderers are the central banks. It is *they* that allow states to borrow from future citizens to pay *today's* debts. One need only look at the National Debt to realize this.

But that's not to say Darkcoins are without issues. A few excellent questions have arisen:

- What if these "Masternodes" eventually form centralization?
- What if Darkcoin is abandoned by the creators once the price goes through the roof?
- Who is trustworthy enough to "audit" Darkcoin? We saw an audit with Truecrypt in 2013 which turned out to show no backdoors... except that the developers shut it down with a cryptic message saying Truecrypt was Not Secure Anymore. We can argue all day about what that meant.

These questions may never be answered. But that should not stop us from forging a new frontier in anonymity services.

Using Darkcoin for Business

IT IS much harder to run a Hidden Tor Service than it is to open a business using Darkcoin. It's so simple really that it boggles the mind what might be available in the future... and with minimal risk to you.

If this appeals to you, then get the Darkcoin Wallet. This is used to send/receive/store Darkcoin with the benefit of using Darksend for 100% anonymity. Most of your patrons will want you to have a wallet, so better to learn it early in the business rather than later.

Pick a Transaction Processor

BELOW ARE a few you can research to your liking. Not every processor will suit everyone just as every bank or credit union will not appeal to everyone. You must judge these yourself, weighing your needs with whatever risk your business entails. I've tried most of these and came away satisfied but like everything else with crypto currency, what works for me may not work for you.

ALTACCEPT
Fees
Transaction: 0.25% + 0.0005 DRK; Withdrawal: 0.01 DRK

COINPAYMENTS
Transaction: 0.50%; Withdrawal: Network transaction fee (TX)

COINTOPAY
Transactions: 0% (coin to coin) 0.5% (coin to fiat); Withdrawal: Network transaction fee (TX)
Transaction: 0.5%; Withdrawal: Included with transaction fee.

DARKCOIN GRAPHICS (COURTESY of the Darkcoin homepage)

After this you should signup to the Merchant Directory.

Then (optionally), do some reading on InstantX. InstantX is a double spend proof instant transaction method via the masternode network. Not exactly light reading, but the more you know...

NO SINGLE ENTITY has control of the entire system. Though the chance of an accident borders on the *not likely*, you need to remember that Darkcoin is still in development and because of that, unforeseen things happen. So a healthy dose of due diligence is required. I suggest only purchasing with money that doesn't break the bank in case bad luck happens upon you.

Frequent backups are mandatory for your wallet, more than Bitcoin since the anonymizing process executes more transactions in the background. If you've ever used Freenet, you know how slow the network can be and how much of a system resource hog anonymity often requires. Thus, make a new backup of your wallet whenever a you hit a coin ceiling.

ELEVEN
TOR HIDDEN SERVICES

How to Setup a Hidden Service on Tor

ONE BENEFIT to using Tor is that it allows you to create hidden services that will mask your identity to other users. In fact, you can have a website that is untraceable to you personally, provided you've taken all security precautions to keep your system updated. Here is an example of an onion site only accessible by using Tor:

HTTP://DUSKGYTLDKXIUQC6.ONION/

NATURALLY YOU CAN'T ACCESS this with your Firefox browser without Tor, hence the "hidden" name.

This chapter will give you the basics on what you need to set up your own Tor hidden service. It's not meant to be all-inclusive that covers everything and the kitchen sink, but only to give you an idea of the technical know-how you need to possess.

STEP ONE: Ensure Tor Works

Follow the directions on installing Tor, securing it against exploits and security vulnerabilities first and foremost.

Each OS has it's own vulnerabilities, with Windows being the worst. I recommend you go with Linux after you've mastered the basics as it gives you more control over Tor and is far more resistant to attacks than Windows.

Now might be a good time to state the obvious, something you've probably realized by now, and that is this: That no two counter-intelligence experts ever do the same thing the same way all the time. There is no red pill that makes it "All Clear." No cheat sheet of Magic Opsec Sauce that everyone can master if they only gulp it down. You can't memorize every organic compound combination in Organic Chemistry. Believe me, I tried. There were far too many.

What you do however is memorize the *general principles*, from which you can derive a solution to every problem that comes about. Anonymity is sometimes like that. Your strengths will not be your neighbor's strengths. Your weaknesses will be different as well. You adapt as you go along, and I can guarantee you your skills as a hobbyist will far exceed those working on the government dole.

STEP TWO: Installing Your Own Web Server

A local web server is the first thing you need to configure. It is a bit more involved than space here allows (without jacking the price).

You also want to keep this local server separate from any other installations that you have to avoid cross-contamination. In fact, you don't want ANY links between your hidden server and your day-to-day computer usage outside Tor.

Your server must be set to disallow any data leaks that might give away your identity. So you must attach the server to localhost only. If you're swapping trade secrets and don't want the boss to know, use a virtual machine to prevent DNS and other data leaks, but only if you can access the physical host yourself. Professional web hosting services (i.e. the Cloud) are a big no-no since it is stupid easy for the admin to snatch your encryption keys from RAM.

Go to http://localhost:8080/ via browser, since that is the portnumber you entered at creation. Copy a text doc to the usual htmlfolder and ensure it copies successfully by logging into the webpage.

CONFIGURATION

Now comes the part where most people quit. Don't worry, it isn't hard. It's just that beginners see these numbers and think "Oh no... math!" and throw the book out the window.

But that's not what you'll do... because you're a *smart cookie*.

First, set your hidden-service to link to your own web-server. You can use Notepad to open your "torrc" file within Tor directory and do a search for the following piece of code:

########### This section is just for location-hidden services ###

As you can see, the hidden services function of Tor is edited out by the "#" sign, where each row relates to a hidden service. HiddenServiceDir is the section that will house all data about your own hidden service. Within this will be the hostname.file. This is where your onion-url will be.

The "HiddenServicePort" allows you to set a decoy port for redirects to throw off any efforts at detecting you. So add these to your torrc file.

HiddenServiceDir /Library/Tor/var/lib/tor/hidden_service/
HiddenServicePort 80 127.0.0.1:8080

Next, alter the HiddenServiceDir to the real directory from which Tor runs.

For Windows, use:

HiddenServiceDir C:\Users\username\Documents\tor\hidden_service
HiddenServicePort 80 127.0.0.1:8080

FOR LINUX:
/home/username/hidden_service/, substituting "username" with whatever you named that directory.

RESTART TOR after saving the Torrc-file and it should be operational. Check your spelling if it throws out any errors.

Now then. Two files are created: the private_key and the hostname; private keys for your hidden service which you should keep under lock and key. The hostname is not your private key, however. You can give this to *anyone* you wish.

A descriptor for the hidden service links to other Tor servers and their respective directories so that Tor users can download it anonymously when they link or access to your hidden server.

OTHER POINTS of note
- Visitors to your hidden service may be able to identify whether your web-server is Thttpd or Apache.
- If your offline 50% of the time, so will your hidden service. Little bits (or lengthy ones, in this case) of data like this are useful to an adversary creating a profile on you.
- It is wiser to create a hidden service on Tor clients versus Tor relays as the relay uptime is visible to the public.
- Be aware that you are not a Node by default. On that point, it is advised to not have a relay running on the same machine as your hidden service as this opens security risks.

Shallot and Scallion Option

YOU ALSO HAVE the option of using Shallot or Scallion. Shallot allows one to create a customized .onion address for a hidden service, such as yyyyynewbietestyyyy.onion

On Running a Hidden Tor Server (and other Opsec Magic Sauce)

Having used Tor for many years, it came as a pleasant surprise to learn how few incidents there were in which the NSA managed to disrupt Tor. And I don't mean spam, either, but rather something that brought large sections of the network to a grinding halt. As it turns out, they're bark is much worse than their bite, especially if one is vigilant with their own secure setup.

The thing is, most Tor users couldn't be bothered. But then most users aren't interested in running a hidden server just as most P2P users don't bother seeding. Most are hit n' run downloaders. They know that as U.S. citizens they stand a good chance of getting sued if they leave their balls out there long enough. So some users opt to not further their own security knowledge. Let the Tor devs do it, they say. Can't be bothered.

Except most of the Tor advice by Tor developers I've read come up woefully inadequate. In fact I find that they aren't paranoid *nearly enough*. It's always been my belief that you can never be sufficiently paranoid as far as protecting your freedom is concerned, since the powers that be want to capture it and bottle it the way a cancer captures control of a cell: One organelle at a time with little of it's environment aware of the slow-boiling attack. To be honest... I suspect they *depend* on apathy and ignorance. And a lot of users gladly oblige.

Mr. Frog, meet boiling pot of water.

So then, what can we do? Well for starters, we can get the right security mindset.

TWELVE

TOR & YOUR RIG

Tor and Your PC

A secure computer is your best defense as the NSA mostly relies on man-in-the-middle attacks and browser exploits that deliver payloads to hidden Tor servers. That said, you should anticipate and expect such an exploit can infiltrate your system at any point. Things like Nits (network bugs), you have to be aware of. Thus the need to adhere to the following:

Use Linux whenever possible. Yes, I know you're comfortable using Windows and think Linux too much of a bother. But you won't if you're ISP is subpoenaed for something you said on Facebook. Something anti-feminist, for instance. So learn to use it.

The powers that be typically target the weakest system and the laziest users. The Tor Browser Bundle for Windows was instrumental in taking down Freedom Hosting and Silk Road because of unpatched vulnerabilities. That, and a few rogue Tor exit nodes patched unsigned Windows packages to spread malware.

If you're new to Linux, look at Linux Mint. If you're experienced, Debian is a good choice. Windows can't be trusted primarily because it is closed-source, but also because malware is more effective on it than Linux. If Linux is out of the question, consider Tails or Whonix as these apps come preconfigured to not allow any outgoing connections to clearnet.

Update Update Update

YOUR PC MUST ALSO BE UPDATED, ALWAYS. Not updating leads to vulnerabilities and exploits such as those in Windows. Optimally, you should ensure Tails is *always* updated each time you use Tor, and avoid any sites that use Java/Javascript/Flash or any kind of scripting as these execute code in ways you cannot see. Use these only in an emergency and never in your home system.

Avoid using cookies wherever possible. Consider installing the Self-Destructing Cookies add-on.

Again, you should not use anything but a portable PC since your home PC is most likely not portable enough to be discarded in a trash can in the event of compromise.

Avoid Google wherever possible. Use DuckDuckGo or Startpage instead for Tor sessions.

Situation Awareness

HERE WE GO AGAIN. But reading things three times often becomes a trigger in the brain later on for taking action, so here it is.

If an agency can monitor your local connection as well as the link you are browsing, then (with sufficient resources) they can apply traffic analysis to pinpoint your real location. Therefore, I recommend you do not use Tor in your residence.

Just to clarify, do not use Tor in your *legal* residence if doing any kind of covert work or anything *illegal* without strict security measures in place; the kind the average Tor user will likely overlook.

Let that other guy learn his lesson. It's a tough break, but better him than you. He's a 19 year old named Jimmy who likes hacking. You're a 32 year old construction guy with two kids and a mortgage. Who has more to lose? Right, you. So study counter-surveillance and counter-forensics like your life depends on it. Because it does!

For enemies of the state-level operations, I would suggest not engaging anything even near your online PC at home. Certainly nothing that makes you think you need Tor to hide it. It may be fine for private browsing but not for someone planning a coup, running an illegal operation (home bible study in Iran, for instance), or trying to disappear.

Be wary of using it in hotels as well, where often there are many cams watching with 24/hr surveillance. That location can be linked to Tor activity.

Do not use Tor more than a day in any specific location. A correlation-attack can be done in less than an hour if a black van is parked nearby--a van you will not see. They may not slap the cuffs on you as you walk out of the cafe that very week, but later they might. Consider the area a toxic dump after a day, regardless if you must travel to the next shop or town.

If you want to get really cloak and dagger about it, have an app running (an MMO, for instance) while you are out and about doing your Tor activity that makes it look like you were home during that time.

THIRTEEN
TOR HIDDEN SERVICES RULES

High Risk, High Reward

CNN, along with FoxNews and a hotbed of other media outlets, has been trumpeting the defeat of certain hidden services for a few years now. It makes for good headlines. Services like Silk Road and Freedom Hosting, which I'm sure you've heard about. They are a easy target for the FBI since hidden services are not high on the list of priorities by Tor developers yet. Same for the NSA.

Both agencies know every trick and hack there is to know about running a hidden service. And so should you. This is not to say you need the expertise to match their team of super hackers, but that you need even more vigilance to run such a service than you do *visiting* such a service.

Priority number one is simple: if you run one, you must own one. They must not be run under somebody else's control if you can help it, because if that service is compromised, *everyone* goes down. That means total anonymity, 100% of the time with world-class jewel-thief stealth ability.

The Silk Road admin did not have this ability. In fact, looking through the online docs detailing the arrest, one gets the impression he was very lax in IT security procedure. He repeatedly made mistakes such that luck on the part of LE never really came into it at all. The guy was just sloppy.

FIRST

Never, ever, ever run a hidden service within a VM that is owned by a friend or a Cloud space provider. Remember, all "The Cloud" is, is someone *else's* drive or network, not your own. Encryption keys can be dumped from RAM. And who owns the RAM?

Right. The Cloud provider. Lightning strikes and there goes your own anonymity as well as the anonymity of your visitors if they are lazy in their browser habits. The FBI delivered a "nit" (network investigative technique) this way to unpatched Tor Browser Bundles in 2013. If, however, you own the machine, then it's a different story. But let's back up a few steps and assume you don't. How might you go about running it on a host system?

Well first off, you would need two separate physical hosts from different parties, both running in virtual machines with a firewall-enabled OS that only allows Tor network activity and *nothing else.*

The second physical host is the one the hidden service runs from, also VM'ed. Secure connections are enabled by IPSec. What's IPSec, you ask?

"IPSec is a protocol suite, for securing Internet Protocol (IP) communications by authenticating and encrypting each IP packet of a communication session. IPsec can be used in protecting data flows between a pair of hosts (host-to-host), between a pair of security gateways (network-to-network), or between a security gateway and a host (network-to-host)."

If an intruder agent tampers with anything, you will know about it and can shut down the service or move it to a safer place, and all while being a ghost in the machine. You can imagine how valuable this would be in North Korea.

If you were in that cesspool of a country, you would be more than a little paranoid if the server went down even for a few seconds. But you could always move it to a more secure location or even start over, and you might just want to since you would not know if a RAID failure had occurred or if some commie jackboot was sending a copy of the VM to the higher ups.

SECOND

If going the host route, you must ensure that remote-console is always available to you by the host, any time you want. You must do everything remotely, in fact, and change passwords frequently via https. I'd say once per day as paranoia in such a climate as North Korea would be good for your health.

THIRD

You must never, not even once, access the service from home. Not from your Nexus 7. Not from your girlfriend's Galaxy Note. Not even via Tor from your backyard using your neighbor's WiFi. Using a VPN as well is risky unless you know what you're doing. Only access it via secure locations at least ten miles away from your residence. Overkill, some might say, but then there is no such thing as overkill in a gulag.

FOURTH

Move the service on occasion. Again, look at any Youtube video on how snipers train to take out an enemy. They move place to place after each shot to conceal the true location from the enemy. How often is up to you. Once a week? Once a month? Personally I'd say every twenty-one days. You can never be too secure when running one of these.

FOURTEEN
DARKNET PERSONAS

"We've been watching you Mr. Anderson, and it seems you've been living... two lives. One of them has a future, and one does not." -- Agent Smith, The Matrix

YOU'VE no doubt read of Tor busts where an undercover agent snagged a phone number or clearnet nic from someone they were targeting because said target trusted too much, too quickly. Take it from Yoda - You can avoid this by retraining yourself, *unlearning* what you've learned.

You must consider your Tor sessions the property of your other

Self. The cloned You - that shadowy thievish looking guy above. The *second* You. One that despises Incubus and loves Tool and views Neo as just another beta-orbiting punk who got the luck of the draw when Morpheus and crew unplugged him. This clone would not use Twitter or YouTube or other social gunk. He would never hang with you nor call you up for a few beers. In fact, he hates beer, preferring J&B as he hacks with John Carpenter's The Thing OST playing as mood music in the background. That's your other *You*. The smarter you.

And he must be the new You *on Tor*. And you must forever separate him from the non-Tor You.

His Facebook, Twitter and YouTube accounts are all fake, having never once used them on his home PC.

His nics are different, as is his passwords, likes/dislikes and even the fonts he uses to browse the Deep Web. Mixing this dark persona with your own would be like the boy made of matter kissing the antimatter girl.

Boom.

Further, any phone calls this person makes is done by prepaid phones that were not purchased by any credit cards he holds. He is a cash n' carry guy and then only if he is twenty miles from home. Any SIM cards he uses are strictly used in conjunction with Tor activity and never used in phones the *other guy* uses. And... he deliberately leaves false info wherever he goes. Kinda like the CIA does.

But to better clarify this idea, let's assume John Doe doesn't know any better. He watches a movie on Netflix. Then he mosies on over to Freenet and drops intel without even realizing it, eager to share his great cinema experience with his darknet buds (no pun).

"Hey guys, just watched a cool flick with Russell Crowe. Kinda Michael Bay-ish and Liam Neeson's cameo was too short, but makes for a good flick if you want to learn how to disappear. But those police, sweet Jesus! Those rent-a-cop guys sure are as dumb as a sack of bricks!"

Police are dumb, he says.

Metadata is collected by Netflix just as it is with Google and Yahoo. Every single user. They know every film you viewed and even which ones you hated. He's even made forum posts indicating similar weather and, though not mentioning names, has griped about local politicians being handcuffed in very geo-specific arrests, even dropping the charges!

How many Netflix fans do you think watched this movie at the time of his Freenet post? How many in cities that had local politicians arrested for embezzling? How many with similar weather depicted in the film? Most likely less than ten. Maybe not even that.

There is also the handwriting element. Does he *mispell* the same words over and over? Throw commas like daggers? Misuse semicolons and run-on sentences? System clock out of sync with his posts? All of this leads to a great profile that ties his IP address to his identity. Often it is enough to get a warrant if he so much as whispers that he's obtained any kind of contraband.

Unless of course, all of this info is tailor-made to fit the other *You*.

We already know that the VPN called Hide-My-Ass as well as Hushmail and Lavabit stabbed their users in the back when threats by a judge became too heated ($5000 a day in Lavabit's case, until they forked over user data). And all this just so they could track Edward Snowden.

Bottom line: Learn from Snowden's mistakes. Take every company's claim of anonymity with a grain of salt. The proof is in the amount of arrests tied to said company or app. In the case of Freenet, none.

But there is always a first time. Recall that they only have to get lucky once, which more often than not relies on your carelessness.

INVISIBILITY TOOLKIT

PREFACE

Winston Churchill once said, "If you find yourself in Hell... keep going."

I can relate to that as easily as you can. But these days Hell itself seems to have taken on an altogether foreign form that is wholly different than the medieval version. These days, many 'angels of light' profess to know what's good for us better than we do ourselves - which is sheer lunacy.

We're not sheep. We all see it. We're not blind. And some of us want to act as beacons of light in a sea of darkness rather than go "Baaaaa!" like sheep to the bloody slaughter. We want to lead others away from the slaughterhouse. But to do that requires a specific set of skills no college teaches.

Skills that will help us turn back the tide of Armageddon on individual sovereignty. Because let's face it, attacks on privacy have increased a thousand-fold. Every day new laws are passed that make privacy as rare as pink diamonds. In the future it just may come to be just as valued as pink diamonds. Do you want to hear your grandkids ask you what it was like in the old days when people weren't monitored 24/7.

Right. Didn't think so.

It's high-time we fought back and fought hard. If you've ever seen the Shawshank Redemption then you know what happens to weaklings - those that don't take action. They get raped again and again and again. Sooner or later you'll know what the meaning of this phrase is: "His judgment cometh and that right soon". It means war. Wouldn't you rather fight before the raping and pillaging starts? I would.

Judgment Day is already here. One cannot walk down the street without meeting a dozen street cams, and as an American/Canadian citizen there are times when I've wanted to disappear from society altogether. Vanish as though I'd slipped Frodo's elvish cloak over my neck and smoothed that runic ring right down my middle finger before flipping off the elites in power.

But first, a little story.

A story way back in 2001, ancient of days and land of vampires and hooded hoodrats wielding double-bladed axes.

Living in close proximity to the housing projects of New Orleans, most days driving back from the University of New Orleans were uneventful. For the most part. Only Mardi Gras seemed to break the monotony along with eating soggy beignets (powdered donuts) on Bourbon Street.

Except for one day in particular while sweating in Manila-like traffic. On that day something terrifying happened. I decided to take a shortcut which turned out to be a shortcut into trouble for no sooner that I sped towards home that a fourteen-year-old girl, black with ripped jeans, red sweatshirt and a nose that could put a bloodhound to shame ran in front of my beat-up Camaro while I drove 15MPH.

I slammed on the brakes and missed her hip by an inch. She slammed her fists on the hood of my car. Boom. Then she flipped me off real casual like this sort of thing happened every time it rained. I hopped out, furious, and proceeded to make sure she knew how damn close she'd come to a date with the grim reaper.

A cacophony of yelling ensued with every color of the rainbows.

Soft swearing, hard swearing, and sweating (mostly me) as she matched every curse word with one better, more deviant, and fueled with twice the rage as though she'd been bred for no other reason than to unleash it all upon me on that fiery summer day. A vampiric Lady Macbeth, this thuggette was. But none of that really mattered to the law. No sir, what mattered was when I grabbed her arm and stabbed a finger into her face as I shouted to be more careful. I began to walk away.

Only I wasn't going anywhere.

Her brother came running. A BIG brother wearing a dozen gold chains and carrying a chain big enough to tie a velociraptor. I swear the guy looked straight out of the A-Team. After that, her mother came screaming and what I presumed at the time was her grandmother, broom in hand (a witch?). I panicked as the big brother threw me to the ground as mama called the cops. I remember expecting a black cat to come along any minute to scratch my face to shreds. I was going down in flames though I was innocent of any abuse.

Fast-forward three weeks later and I'm having my ass handed to me by the most militant feminist judge I'd ever laid eyes on. A real manhater whose harpy-like claws seemed to grow the more I sweat. I had only one choice: Play along. So I kissed ass like I'd never in my whole miserable life. At the end of her screeching rant, I ended up getting off on a technicality. The police had screwed up somewhere, it seemed.

My record was as clean as a babe's arse. Clear as as crystal... or so I thought until later that year a detective came knocking. It seemed that the little girl had disappeared and to my horror, found he knew everything about me. Things that were not in the court transcript. Things I'd done were recorded by various cameras set up around the city. The entire city seemed to be turning a shade Orwellian.

"Talk to me," he said smiling with that shiny badge gleaming. I frowned. Talk to the cops? "Yeah," he replied. "Talk to me or get put on the sex offender's list for abusing that little girl."

Abuse?

I clammed up. Granted, I was native, but not stupid. He ended up letting me go after throwing down every threat imaginable. After that I wanted to vanish even more, and as I would later learn, I wasn't the first to go through such an ordeal.

Up until that point, I'd always trusted the police, or for that matter any kind of higher authority in government. I trusted the media. I trusted newspapers. I trusted juries. About the only thing I never trusted were the palm readers who always set up shop around the French Quarter.

Well, no longer.

From that point on, I swore to myself I'd learn how to be invisible, or die trying. True, I escaped the sex offender registry by keeping my mouth shut. Others have not been so lucky. I've heard another author (Wendy McElroy) relate a similar story:

"Last summer, an Illinois man lost an appeal on his conviction as a sex offender for grabbing the arm of a 14-year-old girl. She had stepped directly in front of his car, causing him to swerve in order to avoid hitting her.

The 28-year-old Fitzroy Barnaby jumped out his car, grabbed her arm and lectured her on how not to get killed. Nothing more occurred. Nevertheless, that one action made him guilty of "the unlawful restraint of a minor," which is a sexual offense in Illinois. Both the jury and judge believed him. Nevertheless, Barnaby went through years of legal proceedings that ended with his name on a sex offender registry, where his photograph and address are publicly available. He must report to authorities. His employment options are severely limited; he cannot live near schools or parks"

Here I was thinking I was the only guy that had experienced such a horrific day. The absurd part is not even that it happened. It's that it is never forgiven. It's never put in the past where mistakes are buried. They are broadcasted forever, branded over and over into our memories. Forgiveness (i.e. granting your past actions invisible to everyone but you and the Almighty) is outlawed.

Well. This book aims to reverse that trend. It aims to give you back your privacy and if you need it, invisibility.

You don't want newspaper reporters sticking mics in your face before you've had your day in court do you? That happened to me. I remember feeling like I'd killed everyone's favorite rock star though I'd never set foot anywhere near the concert.

Think on how your life would change if any of the following happened to you:

- Someone uses your unsecured WiFi to threaten the President.
- A hacker steals your credit card to purchase Russian child porn using proxies.
- You hear sirens just as your phone rings. You pick up to hear a news journalist asking for an interview since you were the last person to see the Governor alive at the Beau Chene Golf and Racquet Country Club (who was later found dead in a pool of blood in the restroom - the same you used!)
- The powers that be are coming after you for child support--without allowing you to see your own children. You try to visit Canada to "get away from it all" for a while, when you are *arrested* at the border. Things get worse when they find a few "manga" comics in your back seat. Manga that is illegal in Canada but not the USA. Chaos ensues. They rip your reputation apart in the name of *the law*.
- Your ten year old brother jokes to his pals on the school yard that he has a shed full of Rambo-like grenades and a few barrels of gunpowder. A girl overhears. She snitches. The cops arrest him (not kidding) but later let him go. Years later, that report shows up when he tries to join the Marines. He is *rejected*. Yes, This really happened to a relative in Louisiana. And that's not to say Louisiana is any better or worse than any other state where hysteria can run amok and drag you along for the ride. The fact is, I'll show you how to prevent crap like this from happening no matter which country you are in.

If you are ever investigated, the authorities will likely tear your place apart looking for anything from which to build a solid case to hand to the prosecutor. Who knows what your situation might be at that time. You might need to go away for a while to strategize with attorneys, maintain your business, speak to family, move assets, etc. It is difficult to do that from a jail cell.

The USA now has a "guilty until proven innocent" legal system. You are not innocent, but I will teach you to gain that precious commodity called TIME which you can use to gather resources to defend yourself.

Resources that go well with becoming **invisible**.

You will learn:

1.) How to be anonymous *offline* as well as on.

2.) How to use your surroundings to lessen risk, special forces style.

3.) How to detect when you are being data-mined: How to hide where you went to school, where you've lived, whom you've loved, whom you did not. Your shopping habits, dating habits, political affiliations. You get the picture.

4.) How to look like a small fish and not a BIG FISH.

But this is just the beginning.

BURN NOTICE & SKIP TRACERS

Burn Notice is one of my favorite TV shows. I don't watch much TV but I do if that show is on. I'd stop to watch it even if a mugger came in and stuck me in the ribs before making off with my wallet. It's that grand. It's thrilling. It's top notch espionage and underground battle-of-the-wits style American James Bond. Sort of like True Lies, but with better looking agents.

The 'burn notice' itself usually comes from an intelligence agency, but can be from any alphabet agency really. It doesn't even need to be on paper. You can get 'The Call' while on a mission in Iran or Brazil or Eastern Europe. What happens is this: The CIA calls you up and at the most inopportune moment tells you they wish to 'wash their hands of you'.

You're done. You're cooked. You're career as an agent is finished.

They cut the umbilical quick and every connection to an agent is severed in true Mission: Impossible fashion. And all for what, you ask? Easy. So they can save face. Any agent has no idea what he did (well maybe a few might have an idea) but he knows he has no work history, no connections, no support and no cash. Poor guy is BURNED. For good.

Well, sort of. If some bigwig at the FBI wants info on him, he can get it from said agency if he has enough pull and the person is a high-value target.

As I watched this show for years I kept thinking: Wouldn't it be great to give yourself your own 'Burn Notice'? Disappear from society altogether? Get a fresh start with new name, new job, the works, in some country where pretty Filipinas fall out of coconut trees as you sit on a beach drinking margaritas?

Well okay, maybe not *that* extravagant. Perhaps it's more simple for you. You want to keep the collector's off your back while you grow a business to pay back your student loans. Start a new relationship. Get away from an abusive wife wielding a double-bladed axe.

It's all rather easy to speculate but difficult to implement. We like our safety nets. We like our 'safe jobs', and a lot of guys don't like losing money in online ventures. So they play it safe. They refuse to take risks. Then one day when they need to leave the country, they can't because they took no action.

Then there are skip tracers to worry about.

Skip tracers? What're those, they ask? From wiki.

Skip tracing tactics may be employed by debt collectors, process servers, bail bond enforcers (bounty hunters), repossession agents, private investigators, attorneys, police detectives, and journalists, or by any person attempting to locate a subject whose contact information is not immediately known. Similar techniques have also been utilized by investigators to locate witnesses in criminal trials.

Before we deal with skip tracers, a word of caution: NEVER fake your own death or disappearance since doing so will bring more heat on you than if you shot Dirty Harry in the ass. Even a simple disappearance can lead to a statewide manhunt, or womanhunt in the case of Leanne Bearden who, after a 2-year globe-trotting vacation, vanished one hot Texas day.

"I'm going for a walk. Be back in one hour!" were her last words. She hung herself from a tree in a wooded area close to her in-laws home. Police helicopters, dogs, and even state troopers spent hundreds of hours looking for her (no suicide note), fearing she'd been snatched and kidnapped. I sat stunned at all the Youtube comments calling for the husband's crucifixion, and all without any evidence he'd done anything.

Don't do this.

Don't kill yourself over bad debts. Don't do it over unemployment (apparently why the woman hung herself). Don't do it over a failed marriage (taken the Red Pill, yet?). Don't fake your own death and try to buy fake IDs from Craigslist. If you try to cross the Canadian border with a fake passport (because we know how nice those border officers are on the Fourth of July with a thousand Canadian-made cars in line to shop), that one guard can ban you for life. Ask George Bush what happened when one tries to cross with a DUI record. He had to get a waiver. But more on this later.

Instead what we want to do is plant false leads that end in Nowhereville for any Skip Tracer hot on your trail. That's what the next few chapters are about. Getting somewhere while leading any skip tracer or other investigator to believe they're on a wild good chase.

A WORLD WIDE WEB OF DECEIT

Your most prized tool in seeking information is also your enemy's most prized tool for seeking your loss of freedom be it handcuffs, garnishments or even asset forfeiture, to which the ATF has turned into a profit-industry. Your neck is out there online as naked as the day you were born.

Being the smart cookie you are, you know it isn't rocket science to vanish online. Lots of guides explain how to cloak your identity using all kinds of tools. Tor for starters. Most computer literate people know of it. Then there's chatting on Freenet. That's not so easy. Then there are VPNs that hide your IP address. You can even chain proxies to post encrypted messages on Usenet with them if you know how to buy services anonymously.

But those guides rarely tell you what pops up when a seasoned skip tracer simply keys in your home phone number or alias into a search engine and starts calling every person you've ever known. That's the part even the encryption experts forget about: That which is right under their very noses. Tracers, like collections, will harass everyone on your city block about you. And boy do they lie. They lie with more skill than the Devil himself!

Aliases

Let's talk about aliases. I'd bet good money that you or your kids use the same alias on Facebook and Twitter that you do on Usenet and The Pirate Bay, or some combination thereof. Maybe something cool like Windsong. You'll switch it up a bit on other sites, maybe go by Windsinger or some such. Oh there might be an extra number or two here and there, but we humans are creatures of habit. We don't like hard work and having multiple *different* aliases for every social media... well some of us just cannot be bothered because that's too much work for us to do. Mistake numero uno.

To prove a point to one of my beautiful nieces in Louisiana, I had her type in a nic she uses on Twitter and P2P. It wasn't just her P2P messages that popped up but those she'd typed on Usenet as well - messages from long dormant times when she was a wee pre-teen. As it turned out, Google indexes Usenet messages from decades ago. I almost felt bad for showing her Usenet at such a young age. And believe me, most of us Usenet guys back then never in a million years believed we'd have 7 year retention rates offered by Usenet farms.

But the real danger was using that same nic across the board on several social media sites.

One website allows you to look up people based on name alone. We found a dozen, yes... a dozen Americans in the south with the exact same name as her but not one with the same nic. Anywhere in social media.

The nic? LinuxGrl.

Any Skip Tracer worth their salt might think she has a nerd gene (she does). She loves coding C++, Java, too. She loves The Matrix and adores the little blonde hacker geek from Jurassic Park like a long lost sister. Any Skip Tracer would find her messages sprawled across the net on every tech forum known to man. She's quite open about her age, too.

When we looked at all the info, it lead a trail right to her bedroom. So many years and so many clues build quite the profile. She freaked out as any red-headed teenager would but only because she feared they might find out which boy she has a crush on.

"Ye gods!" I snapped. "That's all you're worried about?" To which she replied, "What else could happen?"

We were even able to find out from these messages where she meets her fellow high school geeks for PvP Warcraft and Fallout marathons (the pen and paper game, not the PC RPG).

IP ADDRESS SEARCHES

Be cautious about skipping privacy protection if you have an online business. Skip Tracers can execute a simple online WHOIS search that often reveals who owns the domain, which would be *you*. They may even gain your address. If they cannot find the domain owner outright, they may be able to follow clues you've left in your posts. But you'd never be so careless as to leave your real name, right?

Right. But the problem isn't you. The problem is *your relatives. Your friends. Your business associates.* Your ex-lovers. A clever Skip Tracer will lie to fish the info out of them.

And they always sugar-coat it, appearing as someone who wants to help you - an angel of light and niceness and puffy clouds: A prospective employer. A lawyer looking to give away inheritance money (yeah, right). A movie director who wants to offer you the role of a lifetime.

You may hear a lot of affiliate marketers say that it doesn't matter if you have WHOIS protection or not, but I disagree. If you want to shield yourself, and by extension, your freedom (the secret to happiness btw), then you need to not leave a money trail to your front doorstep.

The Courts

Got a speeding ticket recently? That will show up in a public court record. And those records are not difficult to get. Anything that happens on public, tax-funded roads is often available to any Joe Blow who wants it. That includes fender-benders, drug busts and well, anything that involves you pleading to a judge.

A big danger is privately owned property. That is, property that can be taken away from you by the IRS, the Dept of Education, your Uncle Frick who works for the EPA.

Loose lips sink ships. Who else knows about the land but you? Relatives? Friends? How easily can a Skip Tracer contact them about your land--which they so desperately want to buy for a million dollars (oil?)?

Worse, you might be tempted to put this land on a bank loan application as collateral. Don't do that either. Such things are available to the public eye. Not the account numbers mind you but your name and address. If you want to be invisible, don't go taking your elvish cloak off in Mordor where any green-skinned orc can sniff you out and ambush you.

KNOWLEDGE IS POWER

Knowledge is power. Or rather, knowledge is **potential** power. That's the crux of it alright as collectors and skip tracers must rely on your ignorance. In fact they prefer you not know your rights so as to better fuel whatever fear tactics they employ.

Let's say you see the writing on the wall and in six months you will default on a student loan. You feel helpless. You know the collectors will be coming. You know the phone will be ringing. You know they will be calling your employer to harass you and your friends, your family, so what can you do?

Allow me to sound like a broken record: Knowledge is power. They rely on your ignorance and assuming your lender won't work with you and your Ombudsman is fond of Houdini acts, there are a few steps you can take to minimize grief.

If your name/address is scattered over social media like pepper on eggs, then you need to remove it before the slime-skinned collectors get a hold of it.

- Study the FDCPA like your livelihood depends on it (which it does).

Know what they can get away with and what they can't. Remember, knowledge is power. If you wield it, they will respect it

- Check your aliases. Are they the same on every social media website? Is your phone number visible? What about your email? Can a collector or any stranger for that matter view your private info on Facebok? How about Twitter? LinkedIn?

- This above all: ask for any debt or claim to be given in writing. Student loans? Ask for a copy of the promissory note. Often they will NOT have this information. They will give every deadbeat excuse in the world so as not to send it and believe me friend I have heard that ALL:

"We don't have to send that." (A lie)

"We'll send it next week." (Another lie. If that's true, ask her to send you a screenshot)

"You need to setup an automated payment plan first." (BIG LIE)

Always contest the debt and NEVER send a payment until you GET THAT promissory note or bank loan with your signature.

Also, look into these and know what they cannot do

<u>Gramm-Leach Act</u> - Legislation that limits the abuse they can leave on your message machine. Many collectors don't pay heed to this at all. Call them on it!

<u>Fair Debt Collection Practices Act</u>

<u>Telephone Consumer Protection Act</u>

The double-edged sword in all of this is that saying: "Please do not call me again!" This does not work. You must issue this in writing to the bank. It's called a no-contact order. Sometimes it works, sometimes not.

A close friend of mine happened to secure a lucrative deal (by her standards anyway) as an extra on a movie set in Los Angeles. He was an extra with a few speaking lines. Not much to brag about down at Igor's bar but it was a good amount for a day's work: $500. As luck would have it, her effort to pay down her student loan went awry. The collector called her mother and a few friends and managed to get the number of someone on the set. Snakes are clever!

You can imagine what happened.

The whole set had to stop filming to allow her to answer that stupid call. So never underestimate what those hucksters will do to your reputation, and prepare accordingly.

HOW TO CREATE AN ANONYMOUS BANK ACCOUNT

One wintery night when few were paying attention, the Canadian Parliament decided to pass a budget bill containing the single most wicked act of treason in western history.

It's name is FATCA (Short for FATCAT). Developed by Obama, Harry Reid and Nancy Pelosi in 2010 with a fully compliant Democratic Congress, it's workings are the kind of thing a superpower might enact in a sanctions bill against a terrorist state like Iran or North Korea, certainly not Canada. And when you get right down to it, it is an act of financial war - mandating every bank in Canada fork over the financial information of *any* Canadian with US citizenship. It's passed to the Canadian Tax Service, then to the IRS - the same who demand all Canadians with U.S. citizenship to file and/or pay taxes to the US despite not ever living there.

Things like this are a slippery slope to civil wars and revolutions. Worse, the Canadian Parliament did not resist in selling out it's own people. One politician in Parliament claimed "We had no choice as we had thirty days to decide or face a 30% penalty on all investments in the USA."

In other words, they were "just following orders."

Where've we heard that before?

At any rate it seems that Big Brother is alive and well and Judas himself could not have orchestrated a sharper backstab. A few Canadians have filed a federal lawsuit to be sure, claiming it to be unconstitutional (it is), but even if the suit is successful and the law overturned, banks will not be in a hurry to revert their systems as it is so expensive.

But make no mistake: If you are a US citizen, they want to know so as to rat you out to the IRS for not paying taxes in two countries. In essence, for not being a nice little lemming with wrists outstretched. This is a problem for those who love freedom, and by extension, happiness, to say nothing about those who love anonymity.

HIDING ASSETS

If you want to hide valuables from a spouse and do not mind tangible assets, look into opening an anonymous deposit box overseas. It is still technically an "account" but Das Safe, located in Vienna, does a good job of preserving your privacy and demand no ID from you. Bear in mind though that if you lose your key, it's tough to retrieve another one.

Also be aware that anything sitting in an overseas vault is not convenient. It is time-consuming to get it, sell it, convert it to gold or cash and retrieve it and all paying attention to leaving no financial trail. But then financial anonymity has never been cheap. You have to weigh the needs of an emergency to your need of invisibility.

Other Options:

Bitcoin

You can go the Bitcoin route and buy currency, but you will face stiff fees as Paypal is a high-risk method when the two are paired.

And there is a tough learning curve if you're not good with computers. Nevertheless, there are guides that can walk you through it but Bitcoins are not anonymous by themselves.

Ptshamrock

Here you can buy an anonymous debit card and other items. They are legitimate and have been around for years, however are not cheap, nor are they perfect. Blackhat marketers sometimes use them.

Ocra

Ocra outfits offshore investments, trusts and foundations for, as they term it, "Wealth Protection" and "International Business". You may find they offer something you need.

As you can see, there are downsides to just about every facet of anonymous financial accounts. What we have not discussed is *accessing* any of those accounts online. This is dangerous and should be avoided. But (sigh) there are times when you simply must get access to an online account and be secure doing it. Here's how:

1. A VPN (Virtual Private Network). Trial versions abound. You need this to shield yourself from search engines, *not* the government. For that, use Tor. Buy the VPN, the price of which is usually under ten bucks, then install Tor.

2. Tails/Tor downloaded to a memory stick if you're truly paranoid. My Tor book gives details if you want lengthy examples but this above all: never reveal any personal data.

3. Anonymous Debit Card, Loadable. If you load the card with cash, you must not do so within your own town.

STUDENT LOANS

English majors, perhaps more than any other major (except Gender Studies), make up the bulk of criticism for student loan debt. It goes well beyond snide comments made at the office. Politicians have come out slandering liberal arts majors in general but you never hear them criticize STEM degrees, nor do they mention how brutal those programs are when Professor Punjab wants to shrink his incoming Biology class by 85% to free up some research time. We've all heard the usual questions.

"Why did you not study chemistry or engineering? Or go for an MBA? Maybe an M.D.?" they ask you.

Often, these stone-throwers neglect to do any research on these other STEM degrees. If they did, they'd realize that they take out just as much, if not more, debt than their liberal arts brethren. Automation coupled with outsourcing is making *every* degree irrelevant, some faster than others. Even medical students are graduating with $200,000 in student loan debt. That's debt that is neither dischargeable in bankruptcy nor easy to pay off as they:

- Garnish your wages (but not before slandering you to your work colleagues)

- Seize your assets
- Crucify your relationship with your employer

Now it is *everyone's* problem.

The main problem students face, and one we will eradicate, is this: how does one work off the debt without being terrorized? Better yet, how does one make a *fresh start* when they've absolutely exhausted all options save that of stringing themselves up from the nearest tree?

In short, how to disappear at least temporarily so you can grow a business that enables the paying off of said debt? Any businessman will tell you, debt will kill any business. You might be chuckling to hear this, wondering if such a thing is even *possible* for an English major.

"Pay off a student loan to the tune of a hundred grand by... writing, you say? Impossible!"

It most certainly is possible. I know this because my brother did it, but not before teaching him how to keep those baying bloodhounds at bay. Knowledge is 80% of the battle. That is, how to fight back. I showed him. He showed *them*. And I will show *you*.

TAX OFFSETS

Unless you live in Canada, any federally defaulted student loan will likely result in a tax offset by the IRS if it isn't dealt with. Cutting off communication works only if you've got leverage. If not, they take your tax return unless you happen to be self-employed (more on that later). Worse than this is when you are garnished *and* get a tax offset. Let's first discuss what legal options you have.

A few points:

- Your spouse can have her tax return taken as well even if she did not cosign the loan. She *can* however file an injured spouse form and send it to the IRS. Not the best option.

- You can challenge the offset using this site.

https://www.myeddebt.com/borrower/topReviewNavigation

It's difficult and for this to be successful you need to prove validity as to why the offset should not occur. Here are some valid reasons:

1.) You've already paid the debt prior to them kickstarting the offset

2.) You're disabled (not temporarily)

3.) You've recently claimed bankruptcy

4.) You view the debt as unenforceable

Real problems arise when people put off challenging it. They ignore all warning signs and only at the end realize how serious it is. Therefore, *prevention* is paramount if we want to avoid collection agencies.

Prevention: The Department of Education's Worst Enemy

Be aware that if you try to outsmart the Dept of Education, you will have a tough time of establishing a reputation for your business if you want to expand (i.e. borrow money). Anonymity will be your calling card, and you will always be looking over your shoulder in the USA. Problem is, creditors you ask for money don't like anonymity. It may get so difficult that you are tempted to leave for Canada, either to take up a student visa, work visa or to seek permanent residency there.

Other digital nomads have done this and succeeded. They're all over the place in every sense of the word. Some work for Odesk and eLance while others go the affiliate route, but not without jumping major hoops. That should be the last resort since you don't want something preventing you from using your passport.

That said, let's discuss how to prevent an offset so we don't get into that *very long* minefield of red tape.

Consolidation

Assuming you don't qualify for forgiveness, the Direct Loan program can be your ticket out of this mess if you're not too deep in the hole. One option is to group your loans together which would take your loan out of default and put it in good standing. The other is IBR, or Income Based Repayment. If you're making pennies working at 7-Eleven, then you will likely pay nothing. Nada. Zero. But the time to get approved can take one to three months. You can do the math at the link below:

http://www.ibrinfo.org/calculator.php

The other thing to remember about consolidation is that your interest rate must factor into any decisions you make. My advice is to wait until you are out of school before accruing additional loans by consolidation - when the interest rate is locked at a low amount.

Rehabilitation

Many students apply for rehabilitating their loans, which takes nine months. Talk with your lender to work out a payment plan. When the rehab process is complete, default status is changed to good standing. At issue is this: students are eligible for taking out massive student loans (again!) which does not help the situation.

Forbearance: This should be the last bullet in your holster. If all of the above fails, you can put your loan into forbearance. This helps stave off the vampiric collectors but with a terrible price: excessive interest! We're talking biblical revelatory interest here, called capitalized interest that will kill any business before it gets off the ground. Then there are fees the lender likes to tack on. Debt slavery is alive and well.

Those are the legal ways to deal with student loans.

The shady way is to just let them default. If you go this route, they will call and harass you dozens of times per day. They will hound your relatives and friends and colleagues. It will show up on a credit report for a potential employer to see. And that's not even the most absurd part. Want to know what it is?

Okay, here it is: They're not really interested in you paying them back. They're interested in you putting them back into deferral/forbearance so they can charge you insane *interest* (which they fleece the taxpayers to pay).

Bottom line: Pay something. Anything. Even fifty dollars a month. Heck even ten dollars a month by money order is something traceable you can show a judge, heaven forbid it should ever come to that.

SOCIAL SECURITY NUMBERS

If you've ever spent time googling your own name, you know how easy it is to find other people with the same name as you. I googled my own and found a pepper-bearded lawyer in Tennessee with the exact same name that I have. Same age. Same name. Different looks and different jobs. I write for a living. He sues people for a living.

But we have different social security numbers. He probably uses his for just about everything under the sun, including applying for work before he went lawyering up. I don't. Reason being is that I don't like where I sleep and fart being known by every red-headed harpy named Betty who works in HR. So to that I've used a fake address for as long as I remember. When I didn't have the luxury of using my own, I used my friend's address.

As any privacy-minded man should.

Employment

Back in 2008 when Obama took office and the economy nose-dived, I applied in person to some 600 jobs to supplement my income. I must have lost a hundred pounds hitting the pavement. The overwhelming response in 98% of the jobs I applied for?

Apply online.

It mattered not what establishment I went to. FedEx. Home Depot. Publishers. Newspapers. They all said the same thing: Apply online. Apply online. Apply online. I heard those two words so much that I began to see them in my digital alarm clock, blinking like some countdown on a thermonuclear device. Worse was the fact that many asked me for my social number *before* being hired. I found it all appalling and disrespectful of someone's privacy.

Never, ever give this out before you are hired. Doing so will set you in the crosshairs of any collectors/PIs out there looking to gun you down. The two jobs I did secure hired me despite that I'd given an obvious fake social number prior to hiring (1234-56-7890). The interviewer (a man) could have cared less though I did fork over my real one when they said, "Welcome aboard."

Things to Avoid

Universities

When I attended the University of New Orleans, the SSN was used for nearly everything. Checking out books. Scheduling classes. Asking for grade transcripts. I worked in the Financial Aid office and there, too, I found few students were referred to by name. You were just a number. I would call up to schedule an appointment and the first thing they'd say, before anything else:

"What's your social?"

Pathetic.

Even more pathetic was that anyone who worked in the UNO system had access to this number. It mattered not how secure the system was against identity theft because any schmuck who'd just transferred in could work in any department he wanted as long as the work-study money was there. Free money, they called it.

Taxpayer money.

Be careful about throwing this number around like monopoly money.

Class Rosters

This was another biggie.

On my way to the restroom, I happened to notice one professor had every student's SSN beside their name on the class roster. I began to wonder why this was, and if other professors did the same for all other classes. Sadly, there wasn't anything I could really do about this at the time.

Computer Labs

Back when we used a VAX system at UNO (around the time Netscape became popular), we had to use our SSN to login. This same login scheme was how one Harvard student was busted in 2014 when he used Tor to send a bomb threat... out of sheer boredom! Not too bright.

The other threat is that students walking by you in a lab setting can see you type it out. Heck they can even see you from behind since in many labs the chairs are fitted close together to accommodate a sea of new students every semester. Avoid this if you can by logging in from your own laptop.

Grades Listed Outside Class

I was a pre-med gunner before I got smart and quit. In my freshman chem class, grades were posted outside the classroom in the hall, listed with everyone else's social security number. I watched in disarray as many a student slid his finger down the list to see his grade. If I was the nefarious type, it would have been a no-brainer to match the kid with the social number and execute the beginnings of a clever identity theft scheme.

I scratched mine out with a Sharpie marker.

Dorms

My first semester of college had me and my brother lugging my few meager possessions up six floors of my dormitory. But prior to that, I had to check in. Only checking in was done *outdoors*, just outside the entryway.

I had to present my driver's license to show I wasn't some old cajun bum dropout from culinary school to shack up with the girls going to and fro. They checked my name on a paper roster to see which room I had been assigned (I requested a single room... they laughed). And there next to my name was my SSN. Wonderful, I thought. That number again.

There have been a few incidents with SS numbers being stolen over the years and used for all kinds of mischief overseas.

Now you might be thinking, why would someone go to all that trouble? Steal someone else's social security number so they can do... what exactly?

Well, I'll tell you. If you're a criminal, the best thing in the world is to steal someone else's identity. For this reason, you should never, ever use someone else's number. That other person can be on the FBI's Most Wanted list and the day you find that out will be too late without them charging you with identity theft *yourself*.

CHANGING YOUR NAME

Changing Your Name Stateside

Changing your name isn't difficult. It's getting a new SSN that's a pain. It isn't like reaching into a bag of Skittles. More often than not, it's done by a court order. The requirements are beyond strict, placing the burden of proof on you, the ever law-abiding citizen... One being that you must prove to a court of law that you are in danger of losing your life. And you need to *prove* it, not just say it. This might be an abusive spouse who tried to kill you or the FBI's Witness Protection Plan or some such, but the social security number will likely stay with you without this.

Here is what the government says about getting a new SSN.

We do not routinely assign different Social Security numbers. Generally, only the following circumstances are used to assign a different number:

Sequential numbers have been assigned to members of the same family and are causing problems; More than one person has been assigned, or is using, the same number;

An individual has religious or cultural objections to certain numbers or digits in the original number;

A victim of identity theft continues to be disadvantaged by using the original number; or

Situations of harassment, abuse, or life endangerment, including domestic violence, has occurred.

White Lies

Privacy advocates, no matter how careful, cannot get around the SSN requirements on FAFSA forms without risking them saying no. If you use a fake SSN, you can be charged with a felony. So what to do?

What you do is lie to *everyone else*. For instance:

There was a time when I was contacted by a collection agency. TransMediaCorp or some innocuous name. Usually when a collection agency calls, if you listen closely you can hear all the other script monkeys banging away on their keyboards in the background, chatting away (mostly lies). My answer was to lie right back to them.

"Is this Mr. X?" agent Betty asked.

"Mr. Who?" I shot back. (Always, always get them to repeat it!)

She repeated. I feigned deafness. "Say it once more?"

She did and at that point, I corrected her, saying she had the right first name but the wrong *last name*. It was misspelled and mispronounced. I feigned being insulted.

They had the wrong guy. Tough break. She then asked for my SSN. I gave her a false one for the simple reason that as soon as you identify yourself (it is after all the FIRST question they will ask), you paint a blood-red target on your back. They've matched the name with a legal address. From there, it will be one perpetual nightmare after another.

The amount in question was a $500 Perkins student loan I had paid off years earlier, and one that I'd taken on some 25 years ago. But

I wasn't about to tell *her* that. God knows if I did, they might consider the debt paid after I faxed proof of payment, but not before they relayed my name to other collection agencies for *their* databases.

After this episode, I called up every service provider I could think of that held my SSN and had it changed to the fictitious one. Cable company. Electric. Internet Service Provider. It turned out that even the company that mows my lawn had it on file. Who knows how they got it, but only one company gave me grief over the change: the power company. So I handled it in writing, making sure to use plenty of CAPS and BOLD words filled with sound and fury (signifying nothing, now that I think about it). Some people can better sense a bluff over the phone than by mail.

By mail, you can sound like Tony Soprano and if you don't get some action you will send the boys over for a *polite little talk*.

Clone Home

One option you might employ is using a mail service that severs any connection to you. Examples abound of companies you can hire who ask very few questions. A few ask *zero* questions. I've had good experiences with earthclassmail.com, for instance, but there are others if you travel internationally.

Another idea is to check out abandoned houses where you live. Mostly this applies to city dwellers but I have found a few in rural settings, too. Use the address of the abandoned house to have any shipments/mail sent to you there. Just don't go using the same house over and over again.

It probably is a good time to repeat this: Never give out someone else's information on a credit card or loan application. Like, ever. This includes their address. In most first world countries this is a serious crime. Someone somewhere will get burned as one success will lead to another and it will become a habit that is as hard to get rid of as an alcoholic getting rid of margaritas in Maui. It can also destroy any chance you have if, at a later date, you want to legally get rid of debt via bankruptcy.

Lie, but lie responsibly!

PASSPORTS AND CANADA

This is an area I regret having personal experience in. Since 9/11, many systems have been built for inter-departmental communications yet airports *still* have lax security - especially the TSA. Border Stations are an interesting study and I dare say Canadian Border Officers are, fortunately, nothing like their lackluster TSA brethren. What gets flagged at one station gets flagged at them all. It's a little too Orwellian for my taste but I try to be respectful whenever I'm passing through.

If you drop attitude with the Canadian agent at the Niagara Falls crossing, the guard on the other side of the country can (notice I did not say *will*) know about it in minutes if he enters it into the system.

The SSN is tied to your name and employment but does not appear on the passport itself. But a border officer can ban you for LIFE if you lie about any criminal record entering Canada. They locked out George Bush from entering over a DUI he'd received in 1976. Not kidding. He had to get a waiver and that was just to *visit*, not actually move there.

Sneaking in carries risks too, unless you happen to be Nightcrawler from the X-Men and can teleport yourself in the blink of an eye across the Falls. As far as I know, I don't possess this ability.

What can we learn from this?

We can learn not to leave trails.

One option is to not use our passport since it leaves a trail just as visible as the sulfur did for Nightcrawler. But this is not very practical since it makes international travel problematic. Still, sneaking into Canada or into the USA does have its advantages if you have good reason to go off the grid. Many do. In fact, the U.S. border sees more sneak *into* Canada than the other way. From WinnipegPress:

"More people were caught trying to sneak into Canada at remote border points with the United States in 2008 than the other way around, a newly released intelligence report reveals.

It was the second straight year that continental human smuggling and other surreptitious crossings tilted in Canada's direction.

The RCMP attributes the trend to factors including a U.S. crackdown on undocumented workers, more American agents along the border and the shaky state of the U.S. economy. The figures, the latest available, show 952 people were caught entering Canada between legitimate border crossings, while 819 were U.S.-bound. They work at strategic points between border crossings to thwart smugglers of everything from people and drugs to currency and firearms."

Obviously, sneaking across is not a new trend. But let's assume you need to sneak into Canada and need to do it quietly, with no Orwellian tracking system sniffing at your heels. Let's also assume you are going it solo... with no assistance at all.

Without Assistance

Crossing outside of a checkpoint is very easy. Nothing to it in fact. But doing it anonymously, now that's *hard*. Harder in big towns. It's illegal to try and you might not get caught the first time. But most guys will keep doing what they think works the best and then rinse and repeat. If they succeeded on the first try, well dag nabbit they are ingenious! Rinse and repeat.

Bank robbers (usually) don't get caught the first time either. It's when they do it again and again using the same method that gets them caught. Their egos rocket into orbit. They get overconfident. They get cocky. In fact you could apply this trait to most low-level crimes, even non-violent ones like sneaking across.

The border itself looks like a typical power line cut, forests on each side, but the further you get from a town, the less guarded it is. But you should know the ecosystem of whatever area regardless if you plan to hike/drive/fly through because let's face it, it'd be quite a downer to make all that effort only to be the next contestant on Mr. Grizzly's 'You Bet Your Life'.

Most rural spots and undeveloped areas are heavily guarded by movement sensors. Trigger one of those and you'll alert the authorities.

Response time varies significantly, depending on population and distance to the nearest checkpoint and of course, manpower. All the technology in the world does the Borg no good if all of their Borg drones are overworked and stretched to the limit. This is in your favor.

It may be an hour or ten minutes before one arrives. If the latter, you'll walk a little ways before the border patrol drives up. After which you get to meet Officer Simon Sez who carries a semi-automatic rifle along with four of his buddies, one of whom will ask you point blank: "Do you realize where you are, sir?" To which you should state with an innocent smile as you look around, feigning relief that you happened upon this nice Canadian officer: "Hale no sir, I don't believe I do. Can you please tell us?"

Politeness with a dash of respect (*always* saying sir) will win over a Canadian border guard 80% of the time, assuming you're not committing a crime, and you are if you're sneaking across!

But that's if you get lucky. If not, you'll be arrested and deported if you don't have dual-citizenship. Not only will Canadian authorities charge and fine you, so will American authorities. It's a $5000 US fine and criminal record for circumventing a designated border crossing.

With Assistance

Very much the easier of the two since it's not exactly rocket science to get you across the border in either a privately owned plane or smaller-than-usual boat or other watercraft. Better still if you're smuggled in close to a Mohawk native reservation where cigarette smugglers get picked up all the time (and overlooked) by Canadian border officials.

In the event you do try to cross, make sure it's not the 'easy path' others take. It's all an illusion setup by the RCMP to catch you on a well-worn trail. Most people caught do something stupid like crossing at the Silver Lake Road area or farm land close to the Huntingdon/Sumas crossing. Every time I hear of a bust, and the details that come from that bust, I think of what T-Rex hunter Roland said in Jurassic Park: Lost World when he tells Hammond's successor to forget about setting base camp at their present location, a location that's plagued with velociraptors.

"Listen, we're on a game trail and carnivores *hunt* on game trails! Do you want to setup base camp or a buffet?"

Smuggling anything like contraband by way of car is foolish. There are sensors at border crossings. Those include vehicle scanning x-ray machines, chemical sniffers and sniffer dogs. So any attempt to hide in a vehicle heading into Canada just won't work either. The GlobeandMail ironically enough went into further detail on what not to do, even revealing that some hotels along the border are under surveillance for illegal crossers.

Bottom line: Don't ever go into velociraptor territory on the cheap!

ANONYMOUS PHONES

How the FBI Traces Calls

Not every average Joe who loathes the NSA has something illegal to hide, and I'm about as average Joe as you can get. I enjoy shrimp at Red Lobster. I love Mardi Gras in the French Quarter whenever I visit. I play video games with the kids down at the Fun Arcade. And sometimes I conduct business while they play on prepaid phones called burners while the kids play. Burners the NSA doesn't like. In fact they have a real hard time linking those phones to my real identity. It isn't impossible, mind you, only difficult. Since I am not a high-value target, they don't bother. At least, I *hope* they're not bothering.

Now then, you probably already know about MVNOs (Mobile Virtual Network Operators) that allow you to sign up pseudo-anonymously. They ask for no identifying info unless you want to give it to them - but that alone is not enough to thwart the NSA. Phone companies are now required to have the technology to work with law enforcement under the 1994 CALEA law.

Worse still is the fact that despite what appeals courts have said, we still have no real expectation of privacy. Most state law dictate

that as long as one person knows about the recording, it is legal. Note I did not say one other person. Only one person... the one doing the recording. Wiretap laws are a maze of red tape that would make Stalin blush. The counter is this: not everyone uses the same phone.
That's in our favor.

The Cons of Using a Burner

You can pitch it in the trash after use and dissolve any trail to you. That's it, and even then.. as long as you took action to conceal your activity. The Craigslist killer was caught by the FBI visa cell triangulation--the GPS signals from his real phone and prepaid phone came from the same place. He even had it on him when he bought the burner phone. When he killed someone, both phones were easily traced since he had them on him when he committed the crime.

Not so smart, but then most criminals don't get caught the first or second time. They get caught on the *third, fourth* or *fifth* time (remember bank robbers?). The adrenaline rush addicts them to the point they're always looking for the next fix... often without upgrading their skillset.

The MAC address can kill anonymity as well. Like the IP address for computers tied to a network, it can lead right to your front door. There are apps like Macspoofer that aid in preventing this, but they are not perfect.

The Pros of Using a Burner Phone

Number one rule: Do not use it continually for any sensitive business or personal transactions. No more than a few days for something important. If you're on vacation in say, Singapore, and don't want the NSA spying on you and the kids, that's easy. Just switch the SIMs out upon arrival. Same for Philippines, Thailand, etc.

But for something like spying? That's a whole other discussion. One might say, "Well, if I'm running a North Korean spy op, why not bypass any surveillance by having my entire team switch to newly bought phones at the same time?"

The problem with that is then you've created a clear pattern of a group of phones all activating at the same time. You might even get careless and give each operative the same phones. Further, if the police obtain the IMEI code off of the burner, then all SIM links previously attached to the phone are discovered. Good for them. Not for you.

You could even be outwitted if they visit the places they think you will buy the prepaid burners - obtain the IMEI numbers in advance so as to get a search warrant to eavesdrop on you. Boom. And you have to know that not all team members will dispose of the phones after every communiqué.

Problems, problems. So what to do?

Solution:

- Manage two persons responsible for managing all phones
- Buy phones from different locations, different days, different purchasers
- Swap phones out at different intervals from random locations (cell towers)
- Issue to operatives at different dates
- Operatives don't know when phones were activated
- Retire some phones unexpectedly, some sooner, after risky ops for example
- Each Op is given set of other Op's numbers, which changes daily

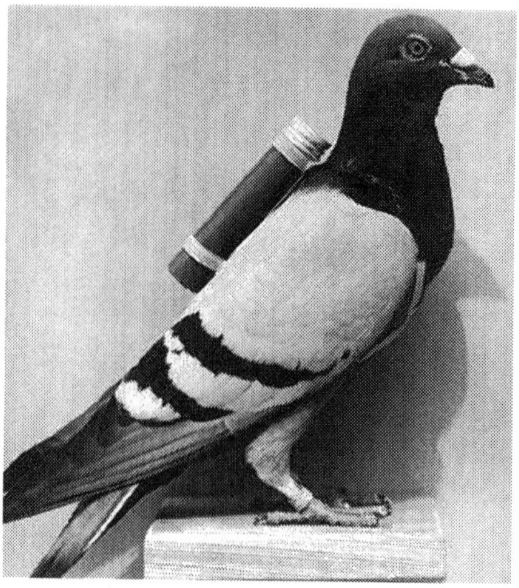

DISAPPEARING FROM SOCIAL MEDIA

Let's cut right to the chase. Social Media did nothing for me but make disappearing harder. With every passing year, Facebook wanted more data on me. More of my favorite childhood cereals (Chocolate Frosted Sugar Bombs, I told them - the favorite of Calvin and Hobbes). More of which movies made me cry. Which made me angry. Which made me cringe (the skeleton reveal in Psycho).

Employers love this about social media. They love that they can google your name and find all kinds of dirt on you from Ars Technica posts to Usenet flame wars you've participated in over the years. Once upon a time, Usenet was sacred. You didn't talk about Usenet. Now it's monitored by Chinese law enforcement. Yet things I wrote ten years back are visible to anyone. My inner child mutant came storming out, fists clenched, teeth gritted and spitting insults before the troll meme became fashionable.

While we can't exactly take a Delorean back to 1985 and start nuking old newsgroup posts, what you can do is take a flamethrower to the media giants who aren't doing your career any favors by allowing your ex to post photos of you so drunk in the French

Quarter that you performed mouth to mouth on a fainted carriage mule who you could swear winked at you as it went down.

Phase 1: Nuking the Sites From Orbit

I nuked my own Facebook account in May of 2010. Little did I know however that it wasn't truly gone. Instead, it went into a kind of hibernation state. Surprise, surprise. Facebook, like Google and LinkedIn and Twitter and YouTube all have this egregious habit of what I call vampire hoodwinking. They lull you into thinking your account is gone, when it really isn't. Nothing is really permanently gone with any of those behemoths. Not Google, Facebook or even LinkedIn. It'd take the fires of Mt. Doom to do to your account what it did to Frodo's ring.

But let's try anyway.

Facebook

Use this link to delete your account.
https://www.facebook.com/help/delete_account

This isn't like tossing out a batch of brownies when you're on a new diet. This effect is (supposedly) permanent. You're not going to get it back. You can't salvage anything for a new account. So contact lists, favorites, bookmarks, posts, pictures are all gone unless you saved them locally to your hard drive or dropbox. Now might be a good time to ask for some awkward pics to be taken down.

Twitter

Follow this to deactivate your Twitter account.
https://twitter.com/settings/account

Like Facebook, once it's gone, it's GONE. But the process takes time. When I deleted one of my pen names, a horror pen that wasn't selling, it took *seven* days and a full moon. I never was good at writing omens.

Google+

For Google, go to the homepage to deactivate.

https://accounts.google.com/Login

This will nuke your Gmail and Youtube accounts as well since they tie everything together, but you can be more selective in what you wish to leave. They call it "Downgrading," but know that your identity might still pop up in search engines.

I have personally found AccountKiller to be of high value here, as there were some accounts still active that I hadn't used in years, but a few that had stored my present phone number and address publicly. *Enhancements*, they claim.

Phase 2: Nuking Criminal and Public Records

Now we come to the area where Skip Tracers love to dig, and dig DEEP. We're talking Gimli's drunken dwarf king deep who loves to delve in places he shouldn't (how'd that turn out for him?).

Without any background information, they will be chasing ghosts and wild geese to who knows where. Bad for them. Good for us. We'll nuke what remnants of our social selves are ripe for the taking -which in the end only hurt *us*, after all. As we go through these, realize this is a very short list and if there is one thing I love about Reddit, it's that they don't believe in short lists.

Here's the major players.

Spokeo - This is the big one. The one every Skip Tracer and collector uses by default. The amount of data they had on me made me want to retch my In n' Out burger! Former email addresses. Relationships. Marriages. Schools. For a few dollars more they'd probably tell a collector if I put ketchup on my fries or on the side. The kind of guys Agent Smith might call up to find where Neo was hiding.

Intelius - I was in this database too, but not for any criminal activity (whew!). Like Spokeo, they keep a lot of data on people without their consent. Not Agent Smith's first choice, but if Spokeo is down... it is. They trawl social media sites as well as keep criminal data. Rumor has it mugshots are on the way. Are Christmas morning pictures next?

Zabasearch - I used this one once to find an old phone number I'd forgotten and didn't want to call up every friend to relay the new one. Later I found that this is *the* site to use if you're a stalker since, after June 2014, emails containing personal info (not searchable by search engines) became publicly available. Ouch.

Going through every site that I'd given my data to over the last ten years was like trying to defect from a vampire clan. Easier said than done. They want something signed in blood. The worst however was hitting *paywalls* and *upsells*. You know, people who claim to save you *money* and *time*.

One site did seem to help shorten time taken to erase myself from the internet. That site is DeleteMe. At $129 bucks, it ain't cheap. But if you're strapped for time and don't mind the fee then it can be worth your while.

Staying Off The Radar

For the next two years you must be consistent with updates. Check those sites every few months for your compliance. Google your name. Your old phone numbers. Old addresses. Old flames. Your identity after all is more valuable to you than it is to them. To them, you're simply a number in a database, and if they had their way, wouldn't mind too terribly the thought of tattooing a number on the back of your neck.

From the moment of Armageddon, I've used Fake Name Generator for many things I do online. You can too. Yes, it does sound like some two-bit app on the Google Play Store that Babu wrote in Bombay one summer's day, but I assure you it isn't. It's quite effective.

If you want free, DISPOSABLE mail, try Mailinator. No signup required. No passwords.

MOBILE APPS

Mobile phones and tablets that use WiFi are devious at hoarding every private detail of your life. Though it's nearly impossible to completely go off-grid with an online smart phone used for business, let's look at some options.

First up, there's Tor Browser

Bet you never knew this was available for Android. This app connects to the anonymous Tor network. Probably overkill for what we wish to do with social media, but helpful for anonymity nuts like me who like the ghost in the machine lifestyle. It spoofs the IP address you use and allows you to mask your own hardware.

Next, there's Spideroak.

If you like cloud-storage *and* privacy, check out Spideroak. It offers "zero-knowledge" security and has end-to-end encryption. The free plan gives you 2GB of storage. It's $10 otherwise for 100GB extra and goes up from there.

Next up is Red Phone. I like this app for it's ease of use whenever I'm in the USA. It secures every call with end-to-end encryption, allowing you privacy and peace of mind. As well it uses WiFi and offers neat upgrades if both callers have RedPhone installed.

It's not perfect, though, but at least it's not as expensive as say, TrustCall. There are convenience issues like lengthy connection times and dropped calls (ever Skype someone from Manila?) so it's not going to be as quick and easy as Jason Bourne does it in foreign locations.

But the pluses outweigh the minuses. I especially love the two-word passphrase as a security feature: If you fear Agent Boris is dead and has been killed by Agent Doris (who now has his phone), you can request she speak the second passphrase. Simple, yet effective.

Lookout - Lookout Security gives you the best protection against theft. Phone lost? You can login to the site at lookout.com to locate where a thief has taken your pone. Data backup is also a nice addition.

CryptoCat - Banned in Iran, Cryptocat is an open-source app that allows encrypted online chat. It employs end-to-end encryption so that you can trust your messages are private. Better still is that it can be used with Tor to *anonymize* your traffic. They also received top scoring in December 2014 on Electronic Frontier's security score benchmark with some stiff competition: ChatSecure, TextSecure, Silent Phone and Silent Text. Reason being is that all messages are not only encrypted, but that you can verify the other guy's identity without the company having access to it.

BullGuard - Bullguard offers anti-theft and backup similar to cryptocat but also offers SIM protections (auto-locks device if SIM is removed), Call Management and Parental Controls (monitors your kids). Mobile security also lets you remotely manage your device.

Orbot - A free app that gives you anonymity with an Android device. I use it for my Galaxy Tab 4. Works well with Tor and wasn't hard to configure for my web browser, email client and Maps.Me app.

Wickr - An instant messenger for iOS & Android, it offers end to end encrypted messages that... self-destruct. Includes file attachments/photos, too. PC Magazine named Wickr an "Editors' Choice for Android secure messaging."

Titanium for PC and Android - Without a doubt my favorite app on my Android tablet for backups.

STALKERS

For some reason stalkers tend to be overwhelmingly male when Hollywood spits them out. I can count the number of female stalker flicks on one hand: Fatal Attraction. Misery. The Crush. Those're the ones I've seen. And they make the male ones look pale by comparison. Stick the knife into poor Jimmy and laugh in his face.

Not exactly realistic, though since they're always a thousand times worse on the silver screen than up close. Most stalkers are your next-door neighbor types. But sometimes, well... sometimes there's an exception. An anomaly if you will that slices to bits any preconceived notion of what a stalker looks and acts like. They break the rules.

What follows is my own story. It's one memory I can't quite seem to delete from my memory banks no matter how hard I try. And lordy, who knows why. Perhaps it's the dark element... the unknown. What COULD have happened. What she could have done had I not taken it as seriously as I did. Even now my fingers hurt from the constant flexing, cracked-knuckle strain I exert as I contemplate the telling of it all.

But I'll leave out the truly disgusting parts in case you've just eaten lunch.

The Bayou Grandma Stalker

The new house I'd rented was as good as any I guessed. Way out there, too, out near the bayou and close to La Place and juuust outside Kenner, Louisiana but far enough from the traffic and airport that it squashed any worries about jet engines overhead. But the mosquitoes, sweet Jesus were they big. Winged vampires with probos so damn big you'd swear you'd been shot in the buttocks with a poison dart like one of them pigmy tribes make.

My father had rented the place to parolees - mostly thieves from what I'd heard. Big time, small time, bank robbers, shoplifters, pimps. Didn't matter what kind. It'd been far enough out of town so as to limit temptation, he'd said, but a couple months passed with no takers. Enter yours truly on a 3-month dry spell in book sales and just generally unemployable for eons.

I still remember his words as he handed me the keys: "Don't turn the place into a dirty whorehouse. Sheriff don't like that." "Whore? What're those?" I asked. He smiled back. That toothless grin of his never put me at ease like it did when I was five, but now I knew how much of a hard ass he was.

I only paid a quarter rent in exchange for repairing the place, but lordy how I loathed crawling under the house to fix *anything*. It wasn't the tarantulas I feared. It was that dadgum Daddy-long-leg spiders that spooked me the most. Mobs! I'd bang out 1000 new words daily (my self-imposed quota at the time) and they'd bang out 10000 baby spiders as I typed the last word. On some dark nights I could swear I heard em popping out under the floorboards like popcorn in a microwave.

Pop-pop-pop-pop-pop-pop.

Then things got louder in July. Peeper frogs amid every god-forsaken bog noise in the universe kept me up. You'd think I'd have gotten use to em, but no. Afternoons were only slightly better. I made a promise to keep busy. I'd survey the property, check mail, repair pipes, try not to sweat too much as it killed my writing mood, when one day I noticed something off.

Some of my mail looked opened. In fact it looked *read*. That feeling, you know? Smudges. Strange scents. Like the kind church ladies wear on Sunday. Letters were out of order, too. Bills were upside down like someone'd repacked them after sticking a cherry bomb into the mailbox.

Humidity. Maybe.

I walked down the lonely road to meet the neighbor I'd put off meeting. A neighbor who lived in a house that *leaned* toward the airport, like the wood wanted to fly off and forever be rid of this frog-infested shithole. Spooky branches prevented this, of course. "You're staying here," the wood seemed to say.

Anyway I knocked and knocked. No answer. Went around back, knocked some more, ridged my forehead and looked around as I wiped away sweat and scratched. The bog seemed far quieter here despite La Place more than living up to its reputation as the Saharan desert of marshes.

I left a note, an invitation for the neighbor to come by and share a beer with me, the new guy (or an iced tea and a Bigfoot flick if a lady). A guy could hope, right?

After heading home I banged out 1500 more words and popped in The Thing as I kicked back a couple of Buds. "Where's Blair?" a voice said into the gloom. Ah, I'd forgotten the electricity had cut out midway the previous Saturday. I ignored the creaky boards under my feet and sank into the couch. Dusty as hell, it was like sinking into a puffy mushroom. The kind some British kids like to play soccer with.

Just when the movie got to the gross "Let's see who's The Thing" blood-test-by-self-inflicted-razor, I heard a noise. I sat up just as, once again, the electricity shut off.

Shit.

Then came a catty sound. Mauling. A yawning slow kind of sound. What the hell?

...scratch....scratch....scraaaaatch.

The door, I thought. I crept to the door over-thinking it as usual. A cat? Not a chance - too slow to be a cat. This was more like a *taunt*. A set of nails being dragged across a chalkboard to grate someone's nerves kind of taunt. My nerves.

I looked out the window. Darkness looked back at me and I started flexing my fingers and cracking my knuckle one-handedly. Think rational. Think logically. But the darkness was so thick it seemed stitched into the clothing of whomever had disturbed me. Intense camouflage. *Whoever* it was standing out there. I could swear I saw *something*. Something frozen so stuff and absolute it was as though dark matter had enveloped it. Despite this, I hated the thought of showing fear by running to get my revolver in the bedroom. No, I thought, and frowned chewing on my bottom lip. I'd face this punky prankster head on.

I swung the screen door open so hard it flew off the hinges.

The monolithic figure was gone. Not a soul stood there, nothing at all but boggy air. I stepped out and as I did waved the fog away. Nothing, absolutely nothing, made a sound. Not even peeper frogs.

A few days later I walked next door once more, determined as ever to find out if my neighbor knew of any rascally kids making mischief in these mossy parts. God knew they had nothing better to do.

This time I met her: a sweet old lady that could never harm a fly. She invited me in. She even made tea and biscuits. A British lady with a midnight cat straight out of Sleepy Hollow. Herself? Liverpool from the sound of it. Who knew but what I did know was that she had a class and a grace I couldn't quite match due to my swampbilly upbringing. I let her prattle on and simply nodded and hmm'ed and smiled rather than allow my lips to leak my ignorance.

French-Acadian lineages was the topic, her *spessscialty* apparently. Not my cup of tea but I listened anyway as she did most of the talking and I just sat there like a bump on a log soaking it all in. And that she did with a vengeance! Talked my ear clean off as frogs croaked outside.

Ten minutes into it, my mind wandered and I noticed a faint lisp. I stared at her wrinkled lips as they quivered and bounced from topic to topic and saw an oddity. No, not her lips. Her *tongue*. Her tongue looked cut. A small one to be sure, right at the tip that affected her speech. Was I seeing things? The day was hot and hazy.

A paper cut? I wondered.

The only time I'd ever done that myself was when I licked an envelope a little too fast.

Lightning struck.

She'd half-assed the licking of my envelopes somehow. When this light bulb bloomed in my head, I noticed her eyes widen and her speech crawl. I coulda sworn I heard her heart speed up as a dark narrative began to unroll in my thoughts. She knew I knew. She had to! It was written right there in her liquid-green eyes.

I excused myself to the restroom and on the way back cut through the kitchen and out of the corner of my eye saw a familiar name next to a Home Sweet Home frame with a few scattered nails. It was an open envelope with my name on it.

I grit my teeth so hard my loose tooth almost popped out. That crinkly old thief!

I paused to rub my chin, my neck, both my eyes. Maybe I was just imagining things, I told myself. Working too hard. Worrying too much. Swamp fever possibly... or perhaps the mailman simply slipped one into the wrong box. I'd done that myself a few times working campus mail back in the day.

But I just couldn't stomach the thought of that old bat, smart as she was, scraping through my mail. Scraping *my* things. Stabbing *my* privacy in the back. Stalking me. And for what reason? So I called her on it in as polite a way as I could fathom yet fully expecting a sincere apology, to which I'd apologize right back.

I was wrong.

Her face *changed* right before my eyes. I thought I was hallucinating at first. That maybe the old witch had poisoned my tea with some dart frog resin. Those sweet, elderly church fingers clenched as she stared at the floor coldly, the paleness of her jaw becoming steely, a kind of veil of jaundice sliding over her face. She seemed to be turning to stone! It was a look I had never seen even in a hardened criminal. A faraway, ancient look, like she'd just celebrated her 2000th birthday and here I was spoiling her party by not outstretching my own wrists. And when she fixed her cataract eyes on me, I nearly bolted for the door right then and there. She noticed this and said,

"Well now, dearie. It seems that you've c--"

Before she could finish, I tipped my old Port Authority cap and exited before she could finish. That was it. I was outta there, permanently.

Later when I asked my father to look into her past, it turned out she was anything but the nice, country granny I'd believed. She'd done time for murder, theft and chronic shoplifting. Oh, and slapping a judge as he sat in Preservation Hall just inside the French Quarter. Just walked right up to him. Brilliant. This on top of the sweet, sugar-coated lies she told me, smiling like a Cheshire cat right into my face.

I was forced to move three days later due to further circus-monkey antics.

The old crone stole my mail as though each and every one of them were sealed with liquid gold.

But there was more. She broke into my house while I vacationed way up in Thunder Bay, Ontario. I'd set up a hidden cam to silence my naysaying father hoping to catch her in the act and send her to the Big House once again with all the other harpies. Only I failed.

She'd spent hours simply rocking back and forth in my living room with her black cat (who kindly relieved himself behind my couch). My father laughed. Pointed, and laughed. But I was determined. I did some more digging.

It turned out she had a son that died a year prior running from police after a robbery. A son with a history of crime with a face *remarkably* like mine. I could sense some residue of reason behind her madness.

Only now I cannot watch John Carpenter's The Thing without smelling that darn cat.

So what did I learn from this? What can *you* learn?

I learned that stalkers come in all sizes and flavors of the rainbow and in all likelihood, will not be a stranger to you. You will know this person personally. They may even be in a relationship with you. Celebrities have the cash to deal with them: Catherine Zeta-Hones and Dave Letterman come to mind. Guys like you and me must use our wits since we're not winning the lottery anytime soon.

The Hitchhiker

In the 1990s I picked up a hitchhiker on my way from New Orleans to a local Mississippi college to inquire about teaching for a semester. It was a long ride. My radio was broken. I could use some nice conversation, I thought. Besides that, he looked like a clean-cut, Leave-It-To-Beaver type. You've seen them: Sharp dresser. Smooth talker. Great big smile with a perfect row of teeth. The perfect guy to sell a Porsche to someone with eight of them already. The kind of guy you'd trust with your daughter in your weekend cabin for the weekend but who'd later break her heart in half, lickety-split. When he got into the car, he smelled like Georgio cologne and cigarettes.

Well we got to talking about everything under the sun. Politics. The weather. The cool new age music on the Weather Channel that he wanted to badly to identify (Pat Metheny, I said). We even talked about Mississippi girls compared to Canadian girls - a world of difference, actually. I asked him what he was studying. His reply?

"I want to be a sorcerer just like my daddy."

I nearly hit a fire hydrant just as a dog was doing his business. By god, I had a male wiccan in my car dressed like Bill Gates.

Before I could laugh at this obvious joke he was playing on me, he proceeded to lay out his whole philosophy of life, real slow and methodical like, waving his fingers around like a magician. I began to ask him questions about this so-called "career." As it turned out, I had to give him personal info about me for every question I asked. Sort of like bartering for dummies. A power thing to him. Personal validation was everything, *as was his image*. I went along with it just as my hands became sweat-filled on the steering wheel and by the time I dropped him off at his destination, I said a little prayer of thanks to the Almighty that the guy never pulled a gun on me.

Would he have? I dunno, maybe. Maybe not.

Bottom line? Appearances are deceptive. That includes: Scents. Visuals. Touch. Audio. Strangers can get into your head and stay there unless you say one word at the outset:

"NO."

Say no to clinginess and control-freaks who'd rather you hang out with them then visit your dying mother in the retirement home.

Now, I was beyond polite with him. A lot of guys I know in Mississippi wouldn't. They'd boot his butt right out as soon as he prattled on about his plans to conquer the world with "Dark Energy." But if you do THAT, you're gonna risk trouble. Be firm, but polite. Don't say, "Get the hell outta my truck, Bozo, before I pump yer gut fulla lead!"

Say, "That's interesting," which I did, to which his reply was: "So do you accept my philosophy, brother?"

(he called me brother the entire trip and it always coincided with him touching my knee)

I feigned ignorance, explaining I needed him to tell me more...

more... more... all the way to the college. It worked. But he did demand my phone number and address at the end. Fake, of course.

Violence ensues if you take the wrong road, and that certainly might have happened if I'd brought his whole self-image crumbling to the ground. Leave the "tough-love" talk for someone else. A judge, maybe.

DISAPPEARING DIFFICULTIES

You might be wondering what it truly takes to do a Houdini-style disappearing act. The answer is this: it depends on how invisible you want to be. There are different levels to it that require different mindsets and experience. You might be invisible one day but goof the next, and now people can see a sliver of an outline as you walk down the street. They may come closer to investigate since invisibility is a power few people wield effectively. Power draws attention. Most people want that attention, if they aren't running like you are.

Another thing it takes, is balls. Fortitude and courage too, but mostly balls because you're not only evading a stalker but his family too since he can call any one of them at any time to aid in the pursuit. That's what law enforcement does with prison escapees - they call for help (unless they're New Yorkers in which case they like to solve the case all by themselves and take all the credit - kinda like Patton).

"*The quicker we clean up this goddamned mess, the quicker we can take a little jaunt against the purple pissing Japs and clean out their nest, too... before the goddamned Marines get all of the credit!*"

Anyway, stalkers take all kinds of forms. Even Stalin was a stalker, lurking in the shadows and waiting to pounce and rip out the heart of anyone rebuking him for slitting throats on the way to the top.

So let's say you are on the run from someone who wants to take your life. Someone far less powerful than Stalin was. Someone you thought was Mr. or Ms. Romantic, before they turned to the Dark Side. The short of it is that you must have a battle plan IN PLACE long before you run. Turning invisible is the easy part. Staying invisible is the hard part.

Actually now that I think about it, let's up the threat a little bit. Forget romance stalkers. Let's say you're on the run from the authorities. If you can master that, you can master anything else since it becomes a hundred times harder if you now have not one, but *dozens* of stalkers who are trained to find people on the run. They don't master pathfinding and detective work in any federal training program, by the way, not even in the ATF which has one of the longest programs for agents. They master it by doing it for years and years and learning from not only their *own* mistakes, but their comrades in other State departments and Federal agencies with which they share strategies of capturing prey.

It's not all gloomy, however. Knowing what the authorities greatest strengths and weaknesses are can help immensely since many get cocky and overconfident after years of success. Can they monitor every train station? Bus depots? Can they shut them down with a court order on the fly? A few can post-9/11. How about gas stations - how many have cameras? Which ones don't? Underground tunnels - can they seal you tight by closing off both ends? You must know all of this before running.

And forget about using even a small airport to jet away.

ID

The other pain the neck is your identity. There's a world of difference between showing a fake ID to a bank to open an account and one that will get you past airport security. So you'll need a fake passport which is expensive (more than a grand in most cities, and you have to know whom to contact).

Do you plan on hoofing it by foot or hitchhiking? This brings a whole new level of risk since you'll stick out even more than you're already sticking out. A stick in the mud with one of those twirly caps.

Think about it. How many hitchhikers did you see last week? If you live near Yosemite or the Appalachian trailer, I'll grant maybe thirty or so. Anywhere else, not so many. Better to rent a car, but you should be picky about it and find a rental outlet that accepts cash deposits. Know that whatever identification you use will be used to run a credit check. More risk.

Sanctuary

Go someplace where American tourists/expats are few and far between. You need not go to Yemen, but consider South America which is filled with nice little getaways to let the heat simmer down. Mexico is a bit too close for comfort (though Yucatan is a nice spot). Many go to Venezuela, but you don't want to stay there forever. Can your parents visit you? Should they, if the evil wizard Foozle is watching them like hawks?

Funds

You run out of money quickly being on the run. So you needs lots of it. Enough to bankroll your hotels as well as gasoline for travel and, let's face it, you don't want to eat Thai food 24/7/365 days a year. I'd say save at least five years worth as this will buy more than you can imagine. This brings up our next topic: Friends.

Friends

There's a saying in Hong Kong about money:
"*When money is stolen you can only beat the dog.*"
Put another way, if you have money - you have *friends*. It's rather Nietzschian to my aged eyes but it is what it is. Sad fact of life, isn't it? About as anti-virtue as you can get. Money indeed does buy friends. And those same friends can help you out in a jam and believe me that jam will come sooner or later. The difference could be whether you sleep in a house or sleep in a cell with mice running over your ankles at night next to Soapy the Bum.

There is a lot to be said about humility and shunning the love of money, but when all is said and done the Almighty might not help you out in this regard if you don't prepare for winter. So get it then, don't procrastinate. Save! Again, you need five years worth if for no other reason than to sleep at night with peace of mind. Worries that stack tend to cloud judgment and contribute to mistakes we wouldn't otherwise have had made if we had green in the bank. You'll also need it to buy intel, but careful about buying intelligence on your enemies since merely *looking* can tip them off if the guy you hired is sloppy.

SECURING YOUR COMPUTER

When I relayed to my grandmother last Christmas that I write books on anonymity and how to become invisible, she nearly gagged on her macadamia nut cookie. I got dead air. I thought maybe I'd given her a heart attack. Then came the lecture. I was going to get arrested by the FBI and every other alphabet agency. I'd be waterboarded. Chipped. Brainwashed. I'd be the next Edward Snowden (though I'm not nearly as handsome).

People, old people especially, tend to group the word anonymity under a pretty big umbrella that includes hackers, spies and contract killers. If you've got an encrypted hard drive, then you've got something to hide, perhaps the location to where you buried Jimmy Hoffa.

"Encryption?" she asked, "I hope you're not hanging around one of those Goodfella guys. Besides, isn't that illegal, dearie? Hm?"

"Not on your life, and thank heavens for small miracles. But I can tell you this:" I reassured, "Even if it were, I'd *still* teach people how to secure their data somehow. Keep it away from snoops."

"But we're all snoops, dear."

"True, but some are more snoopy than others."

"But dearest, I don't want you getting into trouble with the government. They're are friend y'know and they know best (a silent groan from me at this point)."

As we've mentioned before, the last thing you want is for a stalker to grab your laptop while you're in the restroom in a public place. This happened to me on a cold, foggy morning at Wendy's close to the New Orleans French Quarter. Patrons were few and pigeons were still perched on the wires as early as it was. Seemed safe enough. No harm in just leaving my laptop running since all I'd intended was to get in and out of the john, right? My bookbag as well was right beside it. You know what happened next.

Next thing I saw when I walked out of the restroom was a ten year old black kid in grey sweatpants gunning it for the streetcar that went round to the projects; the *worst* place to chase a thief with a car.

But I was determined to get back, 1.) my laptop and 2.) my bookbag that contained the new shrinkwrapped Elder Scrolls game I'd bought from Babbages. Later I recalled being more concerned with the game, such were my hobbled priorities.

So I used my feet and dashed like the wind, chasing him down Canal St. all the way to St. Charles Ave. When I finally caught up with him, the kid swung and slipped from my grasp like one of those kids in the Philippines who can shimmy up a palm tree in 3 seconds flat to avoid a big cat's teeth. Thankfully I was the faster one, at least horizontally. He ended up dropping it. My laptop shattered as it hit the concrete. My grip tightened like a vice around his arm. He snapped at me like I was in the wrong.

"Get the hell offa me 'fore I bust yer face!"

He got off lucky, as did I. As he ran down the street flipping me off, I realized that if he'd been a stalker, an ex-flame, and if my laptop had been unencrypted I'd have been toast. He'd have access to:

- My credit cards
- Login passwords for every tech forum under the sun
- Emails
- Amazon, eBay, Google+, Facebook, etc.

The same can happen to you. Worse case scenario: he steals your laptop then leaves it on your doorstep the next morning with an anonymous sticky note. Something about "feeling guilty." Which is a load of bull since your Alienware laptop is now accursed with a keylogger. The kid wants bank account access. Greedy access.

And that's just identity theft. There are other risks, like getting caught trying to preserve invisibility. Some people just like to stay out of the spotlight for whatever reason. By encrypting your laptop you not only defeat identity thieves, you defeat anyone and everyone that has an interest in seeing you burn.

Tor

I hate to insert a bit of overlap here as some of my other books delve quite deep into Tor territory, but you just can't write a book on invisibility without at least mentioning it. So here goes.

Tor hides the IP address that websites identify you with. No matter where you go on the internet, if you're not using Tor, you're being tracked somehow by someone, somewhere. Usually the big name companies like Coke and Dell and Google. The good news is that it's free. As in, really free. No upselling at all as it's not a commercial product. It is *the* app for anonymity enthusiasts and beginners alike. So much so that the NSA targeted it specifically along with Truecrypt because they were so powerful. So powerful, in fact, that when used together they grant you *complete invisibility* online.

The NSA failed to defeat it. Though that did not stop the FBI from taking a stab at it. They hacked a few websites on the Deep Web by way of browser exploits (or NIT - Network Investigative Technique) that manipulated Javascript to reveal IP addresses. Addresses that lead to your front door. These exploits that have been fixed and it's important to note that you don't need Javascript for the internet to work. Some websites, however, won't work (porn!).

Still, after downloading it from the Tor homepage, you need to ensure via the NoScript addon that Javascript is turned off. This will break some websites that use it heavily like CNN and sites with tons of flash videos. But then if a site is running a dozen scripts it is likely those scripts are tracking you in some way to as to better target you with ads.

Benefits of Tor

1. Immune to Ad Tracking. What you'll see is ads targeted to some guy in Germany or Japan, since the IP will be that of a Tor user's exit relay (Tor users can volunteer as exit nodes if they wish, but it's not mandatory to use Tor).

2. You can surf the Deep Web, aka .onion sites that are not reachable via the regular internet. The downside is little to no moderation. If you remember how 'Wild West' Usenet was back in the 1990s, you'll have a good idea of what it's like. Freenet is also like that, though it does not connect to the Deep Web in the same way Tor does. In fact, it's a whole different Wild West show, which we will go over shortly.

3. Communicate Anonymously. Using Tor, you can say whatever you want in a forum and not have it traced back to the real You. But don't expect all moderators to not take action to ban your account if you step over the line. Yes, I realize I just contradicted myself here. Perhaps it's better to state that there is little moderation rather than no moderation on the Deep Web. But what there is, is moderated by lords of the sith in one flavor or another.

4. Upload to file-sharing sites Anonymously. Sites like those owned

by the former Megaupload founder. If you need to get something to someone without leaving a trace (even if the zip file is encrypted), such is possible with Tor as long as the website does not block it.

Tails

Tails allows you to use Tor and avoid tracking and censorship and in just about any location you could want. It houses its own operating system and is designed for those who don't wish to use their main rig to connect to Tor (though you still can, however if you wish).

You've got several choices at your disposal: You can run it via USB stick, SD or even a DVD. This is pretty handy as strengthens your resistance to viruses. It's also beneficial if you don't want your hard drive to leave remnants of your browsing session. The best part is that it's free and based on Linux *and* comes with chat client, email, office, and browser. Everything the anonymity enthusiast needs to wear Frodo's cloak online.

The downside to using a DVD though, is that you must burn it again each time you update Tails. Not very convenient. So let's install it to USB stick instead.

1.) Download tails installer.

https://tails.boum.org/download/index.en.html

You must first install it somewhere, like a DVD, and THEN clone it the USB stick or SD card.

2.) Click Applications --> Tails --> Tails install to begin the installation.

3.) Choose Clone & Install to install to SD card or USB Memory Stick

4.) Plug in your device, then scan for the device in the Target-Device drop down menu. You'll get a warning about it overwriting anything on the device, blah-blah. Choose yes to confirm the installation.

Tails by itself is quite a powerful tool to use to cloak yourself online. But when combined with an air-tight and secure operating system like Linux, it is virtually *unstoppable*. If you have the luxury of choosing vanilla Tor browser in Windows or using Tails, always go with Tails. Windows has always been the favorite whipping boy of the FBI as well as hackers in general since the number of security holes far outnumber those in Linux.

But Linux doesn't have nearly the amount of supported games. Few supported games = fewer families using it = fewer hackers interested in exploiting it for personal or financial reasons. Them's the breaks.

VPNs

VPN stands for Virtual Private Network. Great for privacy, lousy for anonymity unless you use it in addition to Tor. If you want rock-solid privacy and anonymity (they're not the same thing), then double-wrap.

When I signed up for my first VPN, I was surprised how easy it was. Almost as easy as signing up with my Usenet provider, Astraweb. Only instead of paying $10/month for newsgroups, you pay $10 for a private connection that masks your IP address. You install the app from the service like CloudVPN and connect through that. The VPN can be from any country but if you want subpoena-resistant VPN service that approaches anonymity, you better pick a VPN that resides in a country that isn't known for cooperating with U.S. authorities. No, not Iran. Think France, China or Venezuela. It's not 100% subpoena-proof, but luck favors the prepared.

Freenet

The Big Brother of Tor, Freenet doesn't really hide your IP address. It hides *what you're downloading with your IP address*. Say you want to download a blu-ray movie (not many of those on Freenet, but let's say for argument that you had one you wanted to share). You'd install Freenet. Then the Frost frontend addon (discussed below). Then you'd click the upload button which would give you the Chk address you need to share it with others. Then you'd paste said Chk address to one of the hundreds of Freenet groups available.

Benefits of Using Freenet

Chat anonymously. Freenet is known for it's "Darknet" functions that allow complete anonymous communication between two people or even a group. Upon installtion, you choose the security level. Low security, in which it is easy for others (with sufficient resources) to find your identity, or high security, in which you only connect to darknet peers - friends you absolutely trust. Your files are still encrypted end to end so that no one knows who uploaded or downloaded what.

Download Anonymously. As stated, anything you downloaded, provided you chose normal security levels at installation, will not be viewable by anyone else because of the end-to-end encryption.

Downsides to Using Freenet

1.) Freenet is SLOW. It is not nearly as fast as Bittorrent or eMule. It takes hours to days to download files a gigabyte in size or higher. Plus, if you've an older PC, it is a bit on the resource-intensive side of things, though anything with an i3 cpu and up will be much faster. That's faster resource-wise. Not download speed.

2.) <u>Freenet is complicated.</u> It's not that hard to install and use. It's just hard to find darknet peers you can trust if you want Full Anonymity. The "average" security level is fine for most people, but if you're the leader of a resistance movement in Iran, by all means go perfect dark. Just be certain your darknet peers are 100% trustworthy - a hard feat in this day and age when you've never actually met any of those peers!

3.) <u>Freenet is buggy.</u> It's insanely good at giving you anonymity. Even better than Tor, many say, but you need Java installed for it to work. Because of the sheer complexity of it all, it's not perfect. Yes, Freenet checks whether you have Java on install but even then it occasionally spits out an error if you try to connect. It's usually wrapper-related if on Windows. If this happens, keep trying! Even now, in 2015, I get errors on occasion. I just ignore them and keep hitting 'Connect' until it 'locks on'. Three times is usually enough.

Oh and by the way, never give your Freenet ID to anyone on Freenet. It breaks your anonymity.

<u>Frost</u>

Freenet on its own is unbearably complex to my old eyes. So I was elated when Frost came around. It's a good front end to make reading groups (and downloading CHK files) easier.

Rest assured, there are far more groups then what you see in the above image. This is just the ones available after install - a few I cherry pick just to get things going. You'll have to click the "globe" icon at the top to get a full list, and it will take some time, anywhere from an hour to a day to reveal every single group available.

But first, let's download and install it. It's available at:

http://jtcfrost.sourceforge.net/

Extract the contents into wherever you want to run the application from. If an encrypted container, then you need to have that encrypted container mounted first, then unzip it there.

e.g. Z:\Freenet\Frost

Next create a shortcut to the 'frost.bat' file within. I like to then drag the shortcut to my accessories menu in Windows. Then I disable the annoying splash screen within the Frost options screen.

After that Frost will ask you for an identity nic, something you can use to post messages. This has nothing to do with your IP address, so fear not. It's just a nickname like you'd use for a Usenet posting in a discussion group.

Options

What I do is go into the News2 section in the options page and check to see if "Hide Messages with Trust States" has "Bad" checked. Then I look at the other option: "Don't add boards to known boards list from users with trust states"... I check off Check, Bad, Observe and None (unsigned) so that I don't end up with boards I don't want in the known boards list. Easy, peasy.

Now then. Look in the News1 section and set the "number of days to display." If you want to see what you missed for the last few months, adjust this number accordingly, to say 300 or however far back you want to download. This is wholly different than Usenet, where a group will go as far back as five years automatically.

Trust

You can control what Frost displays and what it does not. Believe me, this is a godsend when you want to ignore or vet certain users. This is done by way of the trust settings coded into Frost itself.

The options are: Trust, Observe, Check, or Bad. If you mark a user to "Trust," then that person can send you encrypted messages and vice-versa in addition to providing missing blocks of data you might happen to need that this person has. The Observe and Check options are simple: Observe means that I will observe that person's behavior until I can make up my mind on whether to trust him or not. Check is the normal state of trust, meaning no decision's been made on their trust state.

Setting a user's trust to BAD will nuke any posts that person makes on any Frost board. That doesn't mean it's nuked from Freenet, as there is no censorship. It's still there, just invisible to my own eyes. I simply won't see his racist rants (of which there are many on Freenet).

Now then. It could be that we've had conversations on Freenet that we don't want the wife to know about, or the police. I spoke with an attorney on here once and I remember thinking that if ever the police were privy to what went on in that conversation, the jig was up. And over a lousy ticket! They'd know my defense before I could even mount it.

Well. Speaking of mounting, that's something we need to implement: We need to encrypt our operating system, or at least at a minimum, our conversation and preferably our Freenet and Frost installation. We do this by way of encrypted containers. If we're trying to disappear and we need to cross the border for example, what we don't want happening is Mr. Groucho the Canadian Border Guard getting angry about wanting to see what we were talking about in that darknet room. Loose lips and all.

I've been back and forth across the Canadian border more times than I can count and if there is one thing I've learned, it's that the personality of border guards are notoriously inconsistent across the board. On Monday you'll get someone with the personality of Super-Grover. That smiley guy could be asked to wear a red cape and he'd salute his supervisors and thank them for the great idea. Then on Tuesday you'll get the border guard no one likes to get: a cross between Animal and those two grumpy old farts in the nosebleed seats of the Muppet Show. He's the kid who was scarred for life when his mint ice cream cone fell over at Disneyland. And now he takes that trauma out on you!

So with that horrid image out of the way, let's discuss encrypted *containers*.

Counter-Forensics

Encrypted containers are easy to store files in. What isn't so easy is learning the application that enables it. But fear not. Truecrypt took me but a mere weekend to figure out and when I did, I kicked myself for not installing it sooner. My earliest thought was that one needed to be an advanced coder of some sort to use it. Maybe one of those so-called NSA superhackers we hear so much about. I was so wrong.

If you can install Windows, you can install Truecrypt. Or Veracrypt or Drivecrypt or Diskcryptor or any variation thereof. They all encrypt your files but have different ways of doing it, and many, many apps are available as you will see. But let's go with the free ones first: Truecrypt and Veracrypt, two excellent choices for us that give a lot of bang for less than a buck.

Truecrypt is first up since the GUI of Veracrypt is practically the same as it's digital brother.

"Hold on a second," you say. "Isn't the NSA involved in undermining Truecrypt?"

Yes and no. It's true from NSA slides leaked that we can see Truecrypt and Tor were in their crosshairs for a long time, but then so is everything else that's tough to crack.

Here's what Veracrypt developers had to say about it. You can interpret it however you wish.

"I am sure the people involved in TrueCrypt couldn't have stayed anonymous and the security agencies knew who they were," he said. "But when you look at the code, you get the idea that these people must have been in their 40s back in 1995. So now they are in their 60s, and they are probably tired or retired."

Truecrypt

There's something else about Truecrypt you might not have heard. It's been discontinued as of 2015, but all the major encryption apps work similarly and it is still secure according to many reliable sources. Once you learn how to use Truecrypt, Veracrypt is a peace of cake. Or you can go ahead and start with Veracrypt. Your choice.

If you choose Truecrypt, you need to know the basics of creating container files. Once you do that, encrypting the OS is simpler. So let's create a container file.

Download the app and install. Create a container file. Think of it as a treasure chest for which you will create a magic password to open it. Being magic, you wouldn't share that password, right? Right. So never share that password.

Here's the quick rundown:

1. After installation, ensure you have enough free space for your container. How big is the data you're putting inside? Blu-Ray size? Set it accordingly.

2. Select "Create new Volume" from the drop-down menu.

3. Now you've two choices: go the standard route or the double-encrypted treasure chest route (Hidden volume), also called **plausible deniability**. For a beginner, let's go with a simple file container since hidden volumes require two passwords and can get a little tricky if you want to store files larger than 4 gigs therein.

4. You'll soon get to a screen where you have to 'Select File'. Click it. Browse to where you want to store this encrypted container soon

to be full of treasure. Don't click on any files yet. Just type in a name in the filename box and choose Save-- We'll add our treasure later.

5. Choose AES for an encryption algorithm. Either is fine but AES has never failed to foil an attacker as it's super strong. The others get hit with performance penalties on slower systems.

6. Choose the size. Don't select a size too small if you're storing your honeymoon HD videos inside.

7. Now comes the password. The longer it is, and more random with letters and numbers and symbols, the stronger the entropy and thus the stronger the pass. Write it down if you must but never forget it. There's no retrieving it if you do.

8. Use your mouse to create a random key, which changes the more you move it. You don't have to do it more than a few seconds. The NSA could spend years and years trying to figure out which direction you moved it first.

9. Now pick a file system, but realize if you're storing big files (4gig and up), you'll need NTFS.

10. You're done! Now just click on the file you initially created. Input the pass, and pick the letter drive you want it to mount to. Then paste in your videos/documents/treasure. You won't be able to delete this container unless you *unmount* it, which can be done on the Truecrypt screen.

Passwords

At this juncture I should probably answer a question I get quite frequently, which is:

"Help me! I forgot my password but... I know 15 out of the 20 or so character string and in order so... uh... what are my chances of hacking it?"

The answer is: Slim to none unless you have access to NSA resources, and even that is a long shot for a long password. Encrypted passwords are stored as "hash" files. When you hash a file, even if you change but ONE character in that string, the hash changes. The same is true of jpegs. Throw a picture into Gimp and apply a cool effect or tweak something small and voila. It's changed. Completely different hash set. Same with encryption.

Evil Maid Attack

Truecrypt, like many other encryption apps, stores your encryption keys in memory ram. A cold boot attack can possibly siphon this if the ram is dumped in the event of a raid or our Jamaican laptop thief gets access to your running operating system. If the former, they can cart off your PC *still running* and freeze the ram sticks *and* dump your keys - which contain your password! The thief, probably not. But an FBI team with a black van parked out front? You can bet the ranch on it. They're used to all kinds of lowlifes using encryption. Tax evaders. Counterfeit operations. Drug runners. Hells Angels gang members using PGP to communicate where the meth lab is.

The takeaway lesson is this: Don't leave your computer running with any encrypted containers mounted, as it will be dead simple to sniff your passwords from your ram. Unless of course, you break them in half - which in and of itself might be a obstruction of justice charge. Ten years ago this might not have been the case but the world we now live in is radically different. It demands vigilance on the part of would-be patriots. Always have a plan B.

Drivecrypt

Drivecrypt brings back a lot of memories, mostly good. It was my first foray into proprietary encryption apps and seemed to offer nothing but good things in those early days.

These days though, there are a few downsides as technology has progressed about the same rate as exploits in the wild. One is that it's closed source and at over $100, it's not cheap. But it's got a great front end and extra goodies if you don't mind paying through the nose. It wasn't for me at the time. For me the bigger issue was if the NSA greased Securstar's palms enough (or threatened) to code in a backdoor for the government. If you visit their homepage, you'll see them swear up and down that that's not the case. In the end you'll have to decide for yourself whether or not they can be trusted. For what it's worth, they're based in Germany, not the USA. But if there were a conspiracy then it wouldn't matter which country they operated in.

If you choose yes, know that the demo they offer does not offer strong encryption - only a weak AES key that gets upgraded to full strength if you buy it. I can't recommend Drivecrypt for these reasons:

1. Closed source
2. Pricey
3. Bruce Schneier, a respected authority on all things security, mentioned in passing after the Snowden leaks that most commercial applications in the USA "...probably have back doors coded into them." Probably, he said, which sounds suspiciously like *certainly* to me. He probably has no more proof of that than I do, but then you don't need to see the code to know using closed-source is a risky endeavor after the NSA (and GCHQ) got caught with their pants down.

Veracrypt

Veracrypt is probably your best bet if Truecrypt has you worried about backdoors. To that, even I have to admit that the account of the strange falling out by the development team had me worried for a time. Rest assured Truecrypt *is* still secure, it's just not *as* secure as other apps, depending wholly on what your security needs are. Plus, later volumes allow you to mount Truecrypt volumes.

So what's so great about it? Well, the developers of Veracrypt emulated the TrueCrypt 7.x code and made it stronger for one thing. Brute forcing is now much more difficult because of the iterations and enhancements added to it. Whenever you encrypt a hard drive partition using Truecrypt, it uses 1000 iterations and 2000 for your containers. But Veracrypt uses a whopping 327,661 of the RIPEMD160 algorithm, which keeps your password and safe contents, well, safe. For encrypted containers? Almost double, at 655,331 iterations of SHA-2 encryption. The only performance penalty comes in at a somewhat slower time to unlock encrypted partitions, a fair tradeoff since it now makes it over three hundred times harder for a hacker to crack by brute force alone.

All of that, plus the user interface looks very similar to Truecrypt, so if you're familiar with that GUI, there's not much of a learning curve at all.

<u>Diskcryptor</u> - With DiskCryptor you can encrypt any disk partitions or even your main system partition. Being open-source, it was intended as a replacement for Drivecrypt Plus Pack (a commercial closed-source app) and PGP full disk encryption. It supports AES-256, Serpent & Twofish algorithms with the encryption key being stores in the first sector of a volume.

<u>Benefits to using DiskCryptor</u> when I compared two different systems:

   - SHA-512 hash algorithm in Windows partitions
   - Quicker boot than Truecrypt or Drivecrypt Plus Pack
   - No mandatory "Create Rescue Disk" like Truecrypt (see <u>workaround</u>)
   - Compiles easier than TC.

<u>Cons to Using Truecrypt</u>

   1.) Discontinued. Probably the best reason to use Veracrypt, though it did pass a security audit which you can read about <u>here</u>.

DiskCryptor as well does not use the same GUI like Truecrypt does, so you'll have to get used to learning a new one. Not a problem for most but I tend to be stubborn about learning new any new GUI.

2.) Limited to RIPEMD-160 hash algorithm for Windows

3.) No support, no future security holes fixed

4.) A few motherboards (Gigabyte's Black Edition line) don't like it.

UPDATE: I must have spent a month trying to figure out why the Linux-like BIOS of my Z97X-UD3H failed to boot after I'd input my TC password. Customer Support laughed as they knew about as much of Truecrypt as they did nuclear waste management (beyond it looking like green radioactive goo leaking from a rusty barrel). In the end I chalked it up to a bad hard drive. THEN a month later, after further investigation, figured it due to having installed Drivecrypt on said hard drive at some point in the past (the demo). So use multiple encryption schemes on the same hard drive with caution.

LibreCrypt

LibreCrypt is open-source disk encryption for Windows and unlike the above, is LUKS compatible (formerly DoxBox). That's a big plus if you like to dual-boot. Even better is that it supports the same plausible deniability that Truecrypt does. It's listed on the features page as "Deniable encryption that protects you from 'rubber hose cryptography' (snicker!). If you don't know what that is, it's something like this...

Other features include:

- Easy to use, with a 'wizard' for creating new 'containers'.

- Full transparent encryption, containers appear as removable disks in Windows Explorer.

- Explorer mode lets you access containers when you don't have administrator permissions.

- Compatible with Linux encryption, Cryptoloop "losetup", dm-

crypt, and LUKS. Linux shell scripts support deniable encryption on Linux.
- Supports smartcards and security tokens.
- Encrypted containers can be a file, a partition, or a whole disk.
- Opens legacy volumes created with FreeOTFE

BORDER OFFICERS AND ENCRYPTED LAPTOPS

Bringing any kind of guns or even knives across the Canadian border is a serious offense - at both ends. Marines have been arrested in Mexico with shotguns in the back of their pickup trucks and northward, cops have been arrested (yes, cops!) for failing to check in handguns. Ever since Marc Lépine shot up a school in Montreal way back in 1989 over what he perceived as feminists ruining his life, Canada has made it 1000 times more difficult to own a firearm.

Not that you'd want to smuggle one in. Canadians are notorious for being friendly to outsiders. It's what lies in the likes of Banff Park or out in the Yukon that demands gun ownership the most: Polar bears. Grizzlies. A few smugglers here and there but they probably will leave you alone if you leave them alone.

And on that topic, smuggling anything into Canada requires cunning unheard of, the likes of which Jabba the Hutt himself was never privy to. It's serious business.

And there's no end to crazy ideas, believe me. Stories in which officers have relayed to their families probably number in the thousands.

One involved a Canadian teenager who, at the border, sobbed

like a little baby when the officer asked him if he had any weapons. Like that 'Father, I confess!' scene from The Godfather, the kid admitted how he'd gotten into some trouble down south at a bachelor party and found himself stuck with a handgun he'd never laid eyes on before. When sent to secondary checkpoint it turned out his gun was a BB gun. His 'friends' had played a delicious joke on him, telling him he'd killed a hooker. HA, good ol' Southern Comfort.

Anyway. Let's discuss bringing laptops across the border and other electronic devices in which said device could easily make or break your attempt at becoming invisible. Namely, what tips them off.

Contrary to popular belief, Border Officers on the Canadian side do not know your entire life history when they scan your passport. When you drive through a Canadian checkpoint, here is what happens:

Your passport is scanned (the part that has all the '<' left arrow symbols) using an international-standard that's easily readable by a CBSA language named IPIL. This searches through law enforcement records such as outstanding warrants, both present and past. Beyond this, there's no time to go through every database with the lineup these guys deal with. It simply takes way too much time as planes land every other day with 1000 Canadians who are eager to get home to some nice Timbits and Poutine.

Therefore, the shortcut to seeing if you're a criminal or not isn't by searching databases, as useful as they are (a seasoned criminal will know how to secure false passports anyway). The way to tell deception is by studying your behavior - Tics. Facial changes. Visual cues (where are you looking? DEA agents study where you look to see if you'll give up the drug location after a raid). Tone. Hesitation. Fidgeting. Sometimes a smuggler will, when pressed with questions by a Sam Elliot lookalike, they get nervous.

If *you* act nervous, the jig is up. And they know the difference between fatigue and nervousness. But for what it's worth, being an absolute jerk to the officer will not put you on any blacklist. They have to let you in as a Canadian since that is what the Canadian Charter dictates. What they don't have to let in is *your stuff*. So what *will* put you on the nasty list? These:

 - Shipping drugs by mail
 - Refusing to report to secondary inspection
 - Lying (aka 'Making a False Declaration' which is admittedly a broad topic, and lies always travel faster than truths: If you lie to one officer in Vancouver, the one at Niagara Falls will know about it)
 - Having *any* bad history at the border

So what else might tip off a BDO?

Not giving up your password. As stated, they'll let *you* through but not your beloved laptop. They do not need a warrant at all to search your phone/Galaxy Tab/Ipad.

So then, encrypt? Yes! By all means but you should have a hidden operating system because you absolutely, unequivocally want to give them *something* that makes you *look like you have nothing to hide*. You don't have to make yourself look like a schmuck. You simply have to look like a professional who values your privacy.

Solution

You need to lock down your data prior to your border arrival. Designate a section of your hard drive so that it's encrypted out of an officer's plain sight and with a second encryption key. There you will store your private files. Do this even if you have full disk encryption. Diskcryptor offers this as well as most older encryption applications like PGP and Drivecrypt.

Border officers aren't forensics experts. They can't go through your Windows or Linux directory to see you've got one encrypted file that's fifty gigs in size, nor that you've got a shortcut to it via menu that says 'Calculator' which even has the stock Windows icon. If they want to "image" your hard drive, that's no sweat off your back as long as your password is good.

Speaking of which, try to drop a symbol in the middle of your password. Mix it up with upper/lowercase with a number. Yes, these are harder to remember. To counter this you can use PasswordSafe.

If you're on the way to the border station from the airport, say from Buffalo, NY to the Canadian Border Station at Niagara Falls, it might be too late to encrypt anything. So do it before you get on the plane. You need to have that decoy ready to show, with *recent* activity in case they want to boot up the OS. It will look suspicious if the decoy OS has not been used in a month. Perhaps not to every customs agent, but there may be one smart cookie in the batch who knows you can have a fake OS.

Store nothing incriminating on that decoy OS. Vanilla bookmarks (no social media) only. A nice backdrop. Not the stock install wallpaper that comes with Windows or Linux. Maybe a picture you took on vacation of all the Latina lovelies.

Once, while coming back from Manila to Canada (a backbreaking 22 hour flight), I stored my encrypted container in my camera, one that the border agent asked for directions to flip through the pics. He saw some beach pics I'd shot in Dumaguete but not the encrypted container on the SD card. They're not going to remove it with 20 cars behind you.

HIDING VALUABLES UNDERGROUND

Things may get to the point where you must hide valuables underground. There's nothing particularly unethical about this, so long as it isn't dead bodies or something like enriched uranium leaking out of barrels. Regardless of what you store, know that anything can happen. You could get get mauled by Rottweilers in a junkyard. Who knows why you'd be there. Maybe looking for spare parts. Maybe to pay Uncle Spanky who runs the place a visit. And then what happens to your cache when you get buried six feet under? Right.

We can avoid a few problems if we follow a few self-imposed rules.

Avoid X Marks the Spot - This is a big one. Never mark the treasure cache spot with anything unnatural. No arrows in trees or painted rocks with bright and yellow smiley faces or mini "Stonehenges." These attract fraternity idiots. Idiots will damage the site - they will move things around when they call up other idiots to come and have a hot dog cookout... just before one of those drunken fools drops his cig near the base of the tree.

Google Earth - Use Google Earth to locate the exact coordinates. Memorize them but do not save it in Google Earth unless your drive is encrypted. And forget about using that Garmen, too. Some models save your history. Obviously this should not be on your property if what you're burying is illegal (or if the IRS can take it). Always assume that someone will find it. Someone with a shiny badge and lots of time to kill.

Insulation! - Take a hard drive apart, say an external one that's dead. See how dry it is? Now re-screw it and fasten. Then freeze it for awhile. After, put it out on the porch and then throw it in the freezer again. Open it a few hours later. Yeah, condensation. Lots of it. This happens to motherboards and ammo alike so bury beneath the frost line since moisture will kill any electrical component.

No Water, No Problems! - Try not to bury valuables near streams, rivers or heaven forbid, swamps. Think "Up" when you think Underground. Escarpments and hills tend to make great spots but only at night unless it's out in the boonies. So do cemeteries (if you own one!). Bury it in a non-populated area with elevation enough that discourages daily visitors.

Bury It Naked - Avoid toting internet items with you whenever you visit your sacred spot. That means: Tablets. Phones. Cameras. Laptops. Ipads. Watches that have WiFi (Apple). That also means ditching your car with the fancy-pants navigation system (one the cops will have fun tearing apart to see where you visited). Bike it if necessary. Silence is golden. To this, what works for me is to think

"Zombies!" since the undead are attracted to loud noises like Camaro engines and big trucks, too. If in doubt, watch Walking Dead, Season 1 where one of the group steals a sport's car and the alarm goes off as he travels up to the hideaway camp. When morning comes, so does the zombie hoarde.

GOING TO EXTREMES

One day, your financial situation just might drive you to this:

Looks tranquil, doesn't it?

Almost like someplace a Bond villain might set up base camp, far away from the eyes of any intelligence agency. I sometimes meditate and dream of what I missed when I was walking along beaches like this not too long ago. Know where it is? I'll give you a hint. It isn't Bora Bora, though the turquoise water certainly does look it. It's the Philippines, and if pictures could relay the Venus-like temps, the salty wind of the sea and the feel of a waif's sticky finger slipping into your pocket to filch your passport, you might think twice about defecting there. A week-long vacation is one thing, but to live there is a whole other world filled to the brim with it's own set of unique challenges.

You could want to leave for any number of reasons, and they're probably all justified. Your student loans might be preventing you from securing employment or getting married. Perhaps you're divorce didn't go quite as stress-free as planned and now you're required to "maintain" your spouse's lifestyle. Or it could be you're just tired of driving down Main Street, USA and always looking over your shoulder for fear of being thrown in the can over a lousy expired brake tag.

There's something I need to tell you about exotic places like this. Something I learned that was ingrained into my very soul.

And it is this: Your problems follow you around like a stray puppy.

No I don't mean your *financial* problems. Over there your student loans won't mean jack. I mean your *personal* issues. Anger management. Jealousy. Wanton vandalism. Piracy. Alcoholism. Cat hoarder/herder. Whatever your ethics, whatever your spiritual weakness, it will not magically change overnight when you leave the West. Don't hightail it to escape a bad habit, be it gambling or drinking or cockfighting. You'll just run in a circle until you tackle the problem headon.

But you might find that you need to get away to an exotic place to heal yourself as you restart your life. That's darn near impossible to do if Betsy from SallieMae loans is constantly harassing your family every hour on the hour and Uncle Frick is threatening to kick you to the curb if they don't stop. That's no way to heal. That's a way to the grim reaper's front door. Now, we all meet death at some point, but there's no reason Betsy needs to accelerate it by giving you a heart attack.

Let's look at some destinations that might give you some time to reset your dreams without the usual distractions.

Philippines

It wasn't the sticker shock of the trip to Philippines that almost had me in tears ($1400) or even the insanely long flight (18 hours). It was the *sweltering* heat I had to deal with. I sweat like a stuck pig and burned like a roasted turkey on a spit under that Manila sun. Being raised in New Orleans was no peace of cake mind you, but even our July heat was nothing compared to this. I began to think some of them only went to Mass to escape it. Who could blame them? Certainly not the Almighty.

But I could see myself adapting, as I know you can, if you don't panic. Keep your wits about you. Think rationally about problems (something that seems lacking in Filipino culture and you'll see this if you use Google Earth to view their city grid layouts.

Life is slower there. Relationships are faster, much faster. By the fourth date your sweetie will be proposing. No lie. If you meet the parents, you're not getting out of her sight, ever, because she knows every filipina will be approaching you en masse.

There are other issues, too. You cannot own a gun. If you're a white single male you will stick out like Marvin Martian in Bunkie, Louisiana. No country is more networked than the Philippines. Gossip reigns supreme because of the social nature of the entire country.

And it really is a third world country in some parts. Lack of electricity. Lack of clean water, with Manila being the worst. But the women, heavens. You'll think you'd time-traveled to Hawaii in 1955. The level of attention I got was insane, and I'm no George Clooney either. I'm about as average Joe as they come. Walking through SM mall (as long as you don't resemble an ogre), you'll have massive numbers of women approaching you. If you are in Davao, Cebu, Dumaguete, or pretty much anywhere except

Manila (crime-ridden) and Zamboanga (terrorist central), this is a fact of life.

Unfortunately this brings unexpected attention where the sweet, endearing Filipinas take lovely selfies of you eating by yourself and post it on Facebook and Twitter and Instagram before joining you. Your stalker may take notice if you use your real name with them. They may even do an image search and start some carnage there.

Solution?

A fake profile and persona if you go this route - different interests that go along with that shiny fake ID and fake last name, fake Facebook. Everything to use with the locals but never the government. A lockbox is useful for this.

Canada

Running to Canada to escape student loan debt is one thing. Running for a crime like "kidnapping" your son is another.

If you want to run to Canada to escape a crime, forget it. It's the last place you want to be unless you happen to be Jeremiah "liver eating" Johnson and know how to trap beaver, scale a mountain and survive in sub-zero freezing temperatures.

That Canadian friendliness we see in John Candy's movies comes at a high price: They will hand you over with a side of Canadian bacon if U.S. authorities demand it. I've lived here for over twelve years and though the Canadian police (Toronto excluded) were far more polite and professional than any of my Cajun brethren down in Louisiana, I've never heard of any cases where they hand out asylum benefits like Willy Wonka bars. In fact, they don't grant asylum to Americans, *period*.

There's a funny scene in the film *Escape From New York* where Van Cleef's character, a real "hang em high" supercop kind of guy, threatens Snake Plisskan with death if he so much as thinks of turning his loaned police glider around and flying off to Canada instead of saving the President of the U.S.A

I nearly cracked a rib laughing as I thought, "How stupid does he think Snake is?"

Canada would dropship poor Snake no matter what crime he'd committed. Oh they'd be nice about it, I'll grant you that. Maybe they'd send him back handcuffed in a coffin filled with a hundred bottles of delicious Canadian maple syrup Han Solo-style. After that, they'd throw in some Tim Horton's donuts. Ol' Van Cleef would've loved that, I'm sure.

So heed this advice: Canada is a no-fly zone if ever you're in serious, deep trouble. They turned over Mark Emery, eminent marijuana activist and he was one of their own.

Remember, just because a country does not have an extradition treaty with the USA does not mean they will not extradite you.

Below is an interesting list, where you will stand a good chance of "disappearing," and in the case of a country like Syria, disappearance can be a whole other world of hurt if you don't have connections.

Afghanistan, Algeria, Andorra, Angola, Armenia, Bahrain, Bangladesh, Belarus, Bosnia, Herzegovina, Brunei, Burkina Faso, Burma, Burundi, Cambodia, Cameroon, Cape Verde, the Central African Republic, Chad, China, Comoros, Congo, Djibouti, Equatorial Guinea, Eritrea, Ethiopia, Gabon, Guinea, Guinea-Bissau, Indonesia, Ivory Coast, Kazakhstan, Kosovo, Kuwait, Laos, Lebanon, Libya, Macedonia, Madagascar, Maldives, Mali, Marshall Islands, Mauritania, Micronesia, Moldova, Mongolia, Montenegro, Morocco, Mozambique, Namibia, Nepal, Niger, Oman, Qatar, Russia, Rwanda, Samoa, São Tomé & Príncipe, Saudi Arabia, Senegal, Serbia, Somalia, Sudan, Syria, Togo, Tunisia, Uganda, Ukraine, United Arab Emirates, Uzbekistan, Vanuatu, Vatican, and Vietnam.

In the case of Cambodia, we saw they quite willingly handed over Pirate Bay founder Gottfrid Svartholm to Sweden.

We saw Edward Snowden run to Russia when the heat was on, catching a flight from Hong Kong and later requesting (and being granted) temporary asylum. We'll see if that pans out in the long term.

Fredrik 'Pirate Bay' Neij's country of choice was Laos, after being sentenced to a whopping one year in a Swedish prison and ordered to pay (gasp) $905,000 in "damages." Laos refused to hand him over. Later in November 2014, Neij was arrested on an Interpol warrant as he attempted to cross into Thailand.

Costa Rica may be another option. There have been a few high-profile cases of runners making it there but do your research beforehand. Know the differences in culture. Know the history of extraditions to your native country. Know how to get out fast if revolution starts. Everything safe costs money so you need to have a substantial savings and a portfolio that is diversified. This is so that no one bank can close your accounts over something like student loans and wipe you out.

Thailand

We left out Thailand in the above list. It's a nice place to run to escape problems. Just not *criminal* problems. Putting aside their extradition treaty with the U.S., for one you need to speak Thai to stay there long term. Forget about what you heard on an expat forum that you can "get by" with English. No matter where you are - Bangkok, Chiang Mai, Phukut, you need the language to get around because it's hard enough being a stranger in a strange land without expecting everyone to know sign language. This is the most glaring difference between Thailand and Philippines, with clothing being somewhat high priced.

Thailand Expenses

Rent is dirt cheap, with some places like Chiang Mai being cheaper than others. Bangkok is where most of the tourists hang out and for good reason. Better food than out in the provincial areas and far more reliable Internet. You can go to the website Numbeo.com to see a breakdown of just what you'd spend if you lived there. For 2015, this is what you'd likely be looking at:

Restaurants (average)
    Meal, Inexpensive Restaurant $1.48
    Meal for 2, Mid-range Restaurant, Three-course $17.81
    McMeal at McDonalds $4.45

Utilities (Monthly)
    Basic (Electricity, Heating, Water, Garbage) for Apartment $107.10
    1 min. of Prepaid Mobile (No Discounts or Plans) 0.04
    Internet (6 Mbps, Unlimited Data, Cable/ADSL) $18.82

Clothing
    1 Pair of Jeans (Levis 501) $84.48
    1 Summer Dress in a Chain Store (Zara, H&M, ...) $53.56
    1 Pair of Nike Running Shoes (Mid-Range) $102.00

Rent Per Month
    Apartment (1 bedroom) in City Center $589.57
    Apartment (1 bedroom) Outside of Center $318.34
    Apartment (3 bedrooms) in City Center $1,746.38

Two things jump out at me when viewing the costs. One is the price for a nice restaurant, obviously targeting out-of-towners. The other is clothing. Clothing there is similar to what you pay in Philippines for electronics. Very expensive for the average Thai, but there are ways around this since you don't have to buy name brands.

All in all, it's possible to live there on $600 USD per month, just not in style.

Religion

This is also in stark contrast to the West, as most Thais are Buddhist. Not only that, the King is considered a kind of sacred entity, a sort of messianic figure, the kind you don't want to cross. If you are in a theater and the king is visible, you'll be required to stand like we do when we salute the flag at a baseball game. Only in America this is totally optional. You can even burn the flag in the States. This confuses the average Thai like no other.

In 2008, a woman visiting Thailand refused to stand in respect to the king's image in a theater just before the film (The Other Boleyn Girl) began. Police had stated she appeared to be quite insane (Naturally only an insane person wouldn't bow or stand to a foreign king, right?)

That's not to say the Thais don't have a sense of humor, for in 2012, Thailand police introduced Hello Kitty armbands as a way to shame certain officers for showing up late or getting too many parking tickets. They discontinued this practice though when the world began to laugh (perhaps this was the whole point?)

That's just two examples of major differences that can cause problems if you don't know the culture. So immerse yourself in a few travel books or forums before you even think of going. You may inadvertently face a prison sentence for the crime of ignorance.

China

China is pretty big and easy to get lost in. Fortunately if you're dead set on running here, you won't have to worry about extradition treaties since mainland China has none with the U.S. This comes in handy for whistleblowers like Snowden who leak classified documents.

China can veto any extradition if it interferes with defense or public policy. It's all a bit murky to be honest. On a technical level, yes, Hong Kong has an extradition treaty with the U.S. but that was before Great Britain gave control of Hong Kong over to the mainland. In interviews, it's been crystal clear even Snowden felt this was just too much of a grey area to risk staying in the country long term. Not that he wanted to stay in Moscow since that was where he was when the passport got yanked (no pun).

Disappearing in China - The Good, The Bad, & The Ugly

This is easier said than done. It's easy to flee there, sure, but hard to disappear. Very hard. Americans abroad tend to acquire an affliction there ten times quicker than even in the Philippines. It's called "Rock Star" affliction. And once you've got it, it's brutally hard to get rid of since the celebrity factor alone hits your ego first. Any thoughts on being a humble little shepherd go out the window after a day or so off the plane.

Ethnic diversity isn't really as widespread in China as some westerners think. You will stick out like Big Bird if you are not Chinese, and if you are of the Dutch blonde hair/blue eyes variety of westerner, you'll be as visible as Big Bird would be traveling with those little green aliens from Toy Story. Believe it.

The picture taking is the most obvious. Cute at first, it will quickly grate on your nerves as many Chinese will ask you, "Take picture of my baby?" many times when you go out and about. Only after three or four of these in a week, you'll begin to suspect a conspiracy. Well, it sort of is. They like your *white skin*, for starters. You'll even get special attention by teenage schoolgirls who will try and spy on you while hoping their giggling girlfriends don't give them away as they twirl their Hello Kitty purses. More conservative areas will yield less obvious giggling (behind curtains instead of telephone poles), but the effect is the same: It's impossible to blend in without actually speaking Chinese and knowing Chinese culture.

Then come the questions. From everyone. In Japan they call them "Gaijin lovers" (foreigner lovers) and these nice yet quirky and strange beings will come up to you in Tokyo (or anywhere else in Japan) and launch wave after wave of data mining questions. In China this happens as regularly as the sun coming up. Again, cute at first but it quickly becomes an annoyance after the twentieth stranger comes up to you and asks:

- Is true all Americans own Glock like John Wayne?
- Is Texas like Seinfeld?
- You have beautiful wife yet? Our city offer you many pretty wives!
- Are alien UFO really in Nevada? (hint: Don't tell them it's in New Mexico)
- You has rose tattoo like all Americans, yes? I can see? (eyes your crotch)
- You has Hells Angels in family? Show photos! (begs you to take out wallet)

Rudeness

Now for some of the bad and the ugly.

This mainly applies to Hong Kong and other metro areas where the ancient god Mammon rules with an iron fist. Bare in mind that not every one is like this. Only a few rotten eggs that spoil it for everyone else. But like I said, when discussing rudeness and the Chinese with an Indian, Pakistani, African or Filipino, they in all likelihood will think of Hong Kong as number one on the list.

Deep breath.

The horking and spitting and public flatulence was bad enough, but worse than this was that few trash cans could be seen anywhere. If there were, I didn't see any (or maybe they're just too expensive). This is in stark contrast to Japan, where throwing your Coke can on the ground is seen as slapping the Prime Minister's face. Japanese love foreigners and they want as many visitors as possible. So for this reason their streets are sparkling clean.

In fact, you'd be hard pressed to even see garbage in a subway or even a busy city street in metro Tokyo.

But in China? Friend you don't know rudeness until you've been down a busy HongKong street at rush hour. Think New York is bad? It's not. Hong Kong is like Seinfeld's "Bizarro World" where up is down and down is up and Superman is evil. And believe me when I say I'm no neat freak. But even I had expectations that had to be adjusted accordingly.

As you may have guessed at this point, rudeness make disappearing problematic. Americans, myself included, tend to go Wyatt Earp when confronted with rudeness overseas. This causes problems for anyone wanting to disappear because it draws massive attention to yourself. Thus, if there is one thing I learned, it's that when in HongKong, turn the cheek if at all possible.

A friend of mine relayed what he'd seen once on a weeknight at a high-end restaurant whereby the waiter, who was obviously nursing a hangover as he applied every other ice cold drink to his forehead in between taking orders, suddenly horked his lunch all over the floor. After cleaning it up, this waiter doesn't bother to go to the restroom to wash up! He simply took a mop to the floor, pushed the bucket back into the corner of the place and resumed taking orders with the same filthy hands he'd horked with. That's pretty tame, though next to other incidents I've heard.

In Hong Kong, the mad rush to earn money there is, well, maddening. Far more than even Wall Street exhibits. People ram right into you in Hong Kong in the middle of the street without blinking. They seem allergic to apologizing. They don't even blink if you slip and fall. They merely continue as if they were a couple of medics getting shot at on the beaches of Normandy and you're in the way. Foreigners have been almost run over by cabs that would've stopped or at least honked had it been New York.

Again, mostly in Hong Kong. Provincial areas are far more hospitable but even there you may find a woman saying you "are too fat" if you've been on a date with her. This isn't rudeness to them. It's just honesty.

COUNTERFEITING

Counterfeit items are everywhere in China. The Philippines unfortunately gets a lot of it sent to them because it's cheaper. Cheap shirts that rip in two weeks. Cheap Chinese electronics (phones, tablets, etc) that break within two months. Iphones that aren't Iphones. Hard drives that seem to have been made from twigs and fish bones that croak after a week of use.

Souvenirs as well are hit and miss. You'll see items sold in antique stores that cost far below what they'd really sell for if they were even 10% authentic. Statuettes fall into this category and it is easy to get suckered. They know how to replicate the look and feel of something old. Something dusty and archaic and webby. They may charge you $100 for something like a vase that they claim is from 8th century China. If that were the case, the price would be closer to ten grand. Not kidding. This goes on all over China, where counterfeit goods fool naive visitors every year. If you're going drop major cash on a statue, ensure it is appraised by someone you trust implicitly *before* laying your cash across the counter.

The Disappearing Act

As you can imagine, the cameras everywhere being pointed in your direction is catastrophic to anonymity. A disguise might prove embarrasing (and possibly attract the attention of law enforcement) if your mustache falls off in front of a crowd of gawking Chinese. They may whisper,

"Is he a spy?"
"Why did he dye his hair?"
"Why she feel need to wear a wig?"
"Should I tell someone?"

This in addition to the fact most of those photos may end up online somewhere. Nevertheless, here are some things you might consider. They've helped me whenever that 'Stranger in a Strange Land' feeling came over me.

I.) <u>Learn a basic level of Chinese</u> and they will forgive just about anything you do short of stealing nuclear launch codes. You can't travel incognito well without it anyway, so learn the basics of how to get around - how to rent cars, hotels, how to read maps, open a savings account, check into a B&B, order a steak at a restaurant... And try to be compassionate with Chinese culture. It is not rude for them to say "You're getting fat!" like it is in America. It's like saying, "You're a little sunburned" to someone Stateside. But it is *very* rude for a Chinese woman on a subway to mutter "hei gue" (black devil) to you if you're black. It's quite the catch-22 if you know Chinese and want to call her out publicly on it. If you do, chances are good her eyes will well up with tears and beg for your forgiveness.

II.) <u>Rock Star Status</u> gets old believe it or not. Read any interview with Steven Tyler or Garth Brooks and you'll see that even those heavyweights grow weary of it after awhile, as will you. To that, don't assume that since everyone is taking *your* picture that it's okay to take everyone *else's* picture. Keeping a low profile is okay but not to the extreme, which may arouse suspicion as well.

III.) Talk With Your Hands - If you don't speak Chinese, don't shoot a pic of a local Chinese guy without doing some sign language to ask first (point to him, then to the camera, then smile).

IV.) Be assertive and say NO when necessary. Learn how to say it in Mandarin and learn not to worry about hurting their feelings. Some Chinese students once asked to snap a picture of me because I am 6'2 and have vampire-white skin (this was just outside the French Quarter near the St. Louis Cathedral). I calmly told them my vampire clan would be upset if they ever found out I was walking around in the daytime since it was against the clan's rules, and likely come after who shot the picture. Their eyes grew as big as dinner plates.
 "Vampires?! Ooh!"
 Snap. Snap. Snap. Snap.

CIA MANIPULATION AND DISAPPEARING

Jason Bourne and James Bond are a bit of a joke to CIA agents. Unrealitsic is being too kind. If agents had half of the gadgets Bond uses, their offices would be filled with resumes from every city in the U.S. But to the rest of us normal guys, there's nothing funny about Bond being sliced in half by a laser or Brosnan resurrecting his heartbeat (Die Another Day).

Well, maybe the latter. A little.

They're spies we want to emulate, fair enough, but sadly a lot of methods of disappearing into thin air don't translate well from the silver screen to reality. In fact, the real deal is often quite different.

What you see in True Lies and the Bourne movies that gets the bad guys usually ends up with a CIA agent shaking his head in the theater. It's just not done that way. Not usually. In the past, CIA techniques relied on deception - deceiving the target's mind with psychology - false trails, leads, and lies, lies, lies, but that's less common today. These days it is about intense networking and analyzing and tracing and focusing, getting as much data as you can and all while being as quiet as a church mouse. Boring stuff for James Cameron and Michael Bay.

Yes, you do learn a lot of survival techniques that, for a few moments, might resemble something Bond did on a bad hair day in Madrid, but it's rare. And if it comes down to you chasing a terrorist mastermind through traffic while riding a horse that leads you to the top of the Marriott, well, forget it. You're beyond sloppy. The visibility factor alone would make world headlines. Attention whoring x 1000 = Mission Failed.

Manipulation Tactics

Back when I ran online ad campaigns (my first business failure), I manipulated people left and right without even realizing it. Every day.

I'd fire up CPV Lab on my server and spend (and lose) thousands running ads for affiliate companies like Neverblue and Clickbank while buying traffic from TrafficVance and LeadImpact. Not cheap, but once I split-tested two ads enough to see my sales skyrocket, I was *hooked*. This was effective manipulation. Giving people what (they think) they need in exchange for something I *wanted*: a nice income stream.

Corporations do this all the time. Sears. Target. Wal-Mart. Best Buy. They're artists at it. But what you find works in the USA might not work in Canada.

Point being? Don't hesitate to manipulate if it's required to keep you invisible. A good CIA agent will have zero problems with manipulation if it means it will push the mission objective *forward* - that is, one step closer to completion. Best Buy does this, and they have pretty atrocious pricing on many items, not the least of which is the worthless extended warranty they pressure you into buying.

So why do more people shop there instead of a smaller PC repair shop? The answer is manipulation, and it isn't that different than what the secretive CIA does. This doesn't mean you have to be a brown-noser. Just know how to manipulate without giving valuable intel about your past away.

Forging Allies

The CIA does not like to make pure enemies. They like to make *allies*. They like to forge alliances. To this end, they spend tons of money on operations that find common ground with pseudo-enemies and accelerate common goals. Suppress the bad and elevate the good, which they hope will turn into a nice, flowery friendship.

Then they send in spies.

The Soviets liked to do it this way, only they employed far more evilness in the implementation of it all. Subversion was the name of their game. Specifically, subversion tactics to undermine the *stability* of a country. The moral fabric if you will. You know, kill patriotism or any kind of idealism that could unify a country against outside enemies. It really mattered little what it was that got under people's skin as long as it drove them to fight each other, and that was good enough.

The KGB defector Yuri Bezmenov relayed this expertly and perhaps as ominously as Jonah did to the inhabitants of Ninevah, but with compassion and a dire warning to the West. Manipulation and deceit are the tools of darkness. Devastatingly effective yet as dangerous to deploy as a suitcase nuke. Eventually, things start falling apart.

He laid it out like a strategic battle plan at Midway in his "Love Letter to America," how everything the KGB did to undermine western democracy and freedom as you know it was put above all else. The interview (from 1983) is quite telling and even shocking in some parts of the telling of it, how the Russians would invite every diplomat to mother Russia, get them drunk, plastered, pickled and primed for a lie, then paint a rosy picture of how pretty and flowery Russia was, both the people and her politicians.

Only it wasn't.

Prisons were turned into nurseries overnight. Spies and liars tricked every reporter that came around shooting for LIFE and Time. Magazine spreads portrayed the entire country as victims of the evil U.S. capitalistic empire, yet Russia bore it all like a messiah wearing a crown of thorns, with smiling faces and vigorous "happy" handshakes living under the benevolent Soviet government.

And we know how that story ended. The Soviet Union broke up. The lesson, I believe, for anyone contemplating disappearing in a free country, is this:

Have Ethics. Have a moral base and keep your manipulation tactics sane so that, Heaven forbid you are caught red-handed, you won't be strung up from the nearest tree by your compatriots. Not to sound too preachy here but, God is watching, after all, and sees what lies in a man's heart. Things that cannot be legislated. Sew your relationships to your advantage, certainly, but don't sacrifice your soul to do so.

HOW THE NSA FINDS ANYONE

Your physical location is easy to track if you're predictable. To that, most of us are. Maybe 90% of us.

Think about it.

We wake up at the same hour and place most days. Wear the same style of clothes every season. Shop at the same retail outlets. Visit the same places come Memorial Day. Date the same type of people even if they aren't our dream dates (for me, redhead librarians with glasses). Married people? Forget it. You're not getting off the NSA radar without good security.

Cell Towers

Cell phone grids are a bit like computers in that they need to know *where you are* in order to "talk" to you. Networked computers, too, need IP addresses. Without 'em, there's *zero* communication since it has nowhere to send the data packets. Same with cell networks. Cell geolocation is required to send you your stuff; Skype, emails, Warcraft pings. Doesn't really matter what kind it is, but know this:

The NSA prefers you favor convenience over security since breaching security is harder for them. If massive numbers of people put convenience above security, well that's all the more power in their hands. They win, you lose.

But triangulation is really nothing new. It's just that now they've refined it, looped it, hacked it and mangled it in such a way that it's now intertwined with emergency services. Case in point: you're a hiker whose dog gets stuck in a cliff crevice with no way back up. Remember what Ben Franklin said about liberty and security?

"*Those who sacrifice a little liberty for security deserve neither.*"

And no two ways about it. It's easy-peasy for the NSA to tap your private data either by listening in or CEO-inked backroom deals. At any rate it's pretty darn easy for them to narrow their scope to a particular GSM phone given the number of towers everywhere. From their lips to your eyes:

"GSM Cell Towers can be <u>used as a physical-geolocation point</u> in relation to a GSM handset of interest."

They also use <u>drones</u>.

DRONES (AND HOW TO DEFEAT THEM)

Above, a U.S. Customs Patrol Drone.

If you're trekking across the border and wondering whether or not you'll see a drone 20,000 feet up, chances are you won't. It isn't just the sheer height of the blasted things that are the problem. It's how easily Mother Nature tends to obscure their flight patterns with clouds, fog, and thunderstorms, making any anti-drone technology an exercise in frustration. This in addition that they fly soundless. Silent killers in the night sky. How would you know a twinkling star from one flying overhead?

But fear not, there are a few measures we can deploy, er *employ*.

1.) <u>Sensor Disruption</u> - Any technology with sensors needs to see the target it's trying to capture. So give it a dose of it's own medicine: lasers. Ever wonder why a kid with a laser-pointer gets a visit from the FBI when he points it at the cockpit of a 747 flying overhead? Right - the laser disrupts not only the instruments onboard but the visibility of the pilots. Blind pilots cannot fly straight nor can they read their navigation systems. Same with drones, and though pilot-less, have cameras that relay images to a set of human eyeballs. The downside of course is that you make it all too obvious that you're not some kid with the kitty's laser-pointer.

2.) <u>Hacking</u> - This is far easier said than done. It used to be that drones could be hacked just as flight navigation systems on a 747 can be hacked, but it's harder to do now with encryption. The movie Interstellar goofed. Matthew McConaughey's character (with his daughter's help) hack into a drone flying overhead from years ago. Only it looks all too easy because there is no encryption to hack past. Years prior to the film's release, North Korea and Iran both claimed to have downed drones using hacking techniques whereby they "spoof" the GPS signal and, as irony would have it, send it on a suicidal death spiral.

3.) <u>EMP Pulse</u> - The problem with this is that even if you could create this by yourself, the pulse cares not a whit about your own electronic equipment or grid. So it'd be like shooting yourself in the foot. Actually, worse. Recall the MAD tactic (mutually assured destruction) Trinity used in The Matrix just as the A.I machines were drilling into the Morpheus' ship: The Nebuchadnezzar, with Neo and Morpheus still jacked in. She hit the switch and fried every bot but left her ship defenseless. They all lived, however, an in the end it may just come to that for us.

4.) <u>Counter-Drones</u> - This requires downed drones, of course, unless you manufacture your own. Set these drones to survey the skies for unfriendlies and scan and identify via encryption keys the same way that PGP users do over the internet. The issue of course is that the enemy can see these just as you can see theirs... unless you've got decoys set up to give off fake heat signatures.

5.) <u>Occupy The High Ground</u> - For this to work you'd need teams specially trained and camouflaged to lookout for drones all day, all night, armed with microwave-type weaponry. The microwave itself
    You'd also need powerful scopes to distinguish a drone from a plane which is not discernable to the naked eye even from high up. As well, noise-sensors would be required that detect the low-hum engine noise from a drone, assuming of course you knew the make/model of said drone.

6.) <u>Camouflage</u> - No I don't mean like the Ghillie suit used in Call of Duty 4, but rather the natural camouflage given by large structures. Shadows, bridges covered in vines, that sort of thing. Just remember that traveling at night is risky no matter what you're wearing since the drone will detect your heat signature anyway. Better to stick to tunnels, under bridges, railroad tracks and moving building to building, cover to cover as a disguise had other uses. This is of course assuming you know how to travel incognito as you might be in enemy territory. If you can blend in with what the drone considers 'non-adversaries', then it will not be able to distinguish between you and Vladmir. The downside is if that drone is using facial recognition tech, whereby they can match your face with what they have on file. If you're a wanted man, better wear a hood, makeup, beard or whatever you need to look thinner or fatter than you really are. That also goes for your voice. Learn accents because advanced Voice DNA technology is willing and able to turn you in.

7.) <u>Radar</u> - This is the expensive option. But at thirty thousand feet, you're not going to see a drone without expensive equipment and if you're dropping money like Ebenezer Scrooge, well you might as well go all the way.

Even if you were to step outdoors and see a trail from a jet liner, it will be as a tiny sliver even on a clear, sunny day. Rain and fog? Forget it. So you need radar installations that are secret enough to evade enemy detection but close enough to see the enemy. Quite the catch-22. Detecting the drone is easier than detecting it anonymously. There are CO_2 infrared lasers you can buy from various internet outlets.

8.) <u>Civilian Patriots</u> - Obvious perhaps, as there are over a million gun owners in North America, but it is unlikely that drones will be turned against the populace en masse anytime soon since they must be rearmed and refueled, and a patriotic force would seize this opportunity to string the pilots up from the nearest tree. And believe me, they would find them *quickly*.

But drone *spying* is different than a drone *firing*. And in the end, perhaps that is really all they want - to launch a hundred thousand drones to spy on everyone without ever firing a shot, because when you know where someone is 24/7, what restaurant they eat at, what ballgames they attend and whether they put their ketchup on top of their fries or on the side, well, they don't really need to fire from the skies, do they?

ONLINE FOOTPRINTS

The NSA collects IP addresses like ants collect food. It's a nice analogy, isn't it? They store whatever they can get, usually from apps that bypass security and provide you with convenience. Apple and Samsung made their fortunes this way - convenience above all. Thus many phone apps not only send your IP address which is correlated with Facebook and Skype, but your login locations: cafes, libraries, etc., with the times you did. Thus everyone's digital fingerprint is stored. Well, most people's. If you're one of the ones that are tracked, read on, because we're about to put a stop to that nonsense.

Fortunately, an IP address is not a person *yet*. On that topic, ask yourself this: how might their power be enhanced if everyone did have their own unique number, say like those in Germany, 1938? To login? To send email? To play online games?

I walked into a free WiFi on a trip to California a few years back. A few kids had managed to play World of Warcraft despite the posted rules of NO GAMING during school hours. Well, the NSA certainly knows which games their playing, and who played them at which hour if they decide to go the subpoena route. This is how the NSA finds people who want to disappear.

People on the run forget the digital trail they've already established for years. The NSA hasn't. Sites you've visited. Calls you've made. Friends you've unfriended. They know about them all. So if you want to put an end to this, you must forge a new identity that muddles up the former digital *you*.

And no, turning off the cell won't help. Neither will popping out the SIM because the NSA already has the network map for that WiFi area. The only exception to this would be if you were in Syria.

Bin Laden's Courier

Sheikh Abu Ahmed was not an easy man to find. The CIA spent a year tracking him down, and Bin Laden's rule of no calls or laptops made it all the more difficult. So difficult in fact, that they had to rely on getting intel out of prisoners.

The big break, however, came in 2010 when Ahmed broke Bin Laden's rule by talking about him on, you guessed it, a *cell phone*. Intelligence agencies were already monitoring who he was talking to. When Bin Laden's name came up, the call led them straight to the Pakistani town called Abbottabad.

You probably know the rest.

Soon thereafter, Navy SEALs stormed the compound with 18 foot walls and barbed wire. They were in and out in under 40 minutes and met little resistance. There were no guards or schedules. No guard dogs. No field of tripmines and no Barrett .50 caliber guns to worry about. Not much in the way of fortification that couldn't be easily defeated with a moderately trained infantry. Or a sledgehammer in the case of one SEAL.

The takeaway here is that you don't want to draw attention to yourself by being loud. If you want to truly disappear, don't be a bar braggart. Bin Laden, for all his demonic activity, had this part right. C4 is loud. Mines are suicidal. Tripwires can kill your own and sentry guards are visible from the sky. They're also notoriously loose-lipped as they gossip to kill time.

Despite knowing all this, I watched Zero Dark Thirty expecting the worst. I facepalmed several times due to how loud the actors playing the Navy SEALs were.

"Shut up you fools or someone'll hear! Stop chattering!"

Bin laden was smart. Prime evil, but smart.

Chatter breaks anonymity faster than a maggot spoils rotten meat, and sometimes Hollywood gets it wrong. Those SEALS (the real ones) knew how to be silent. In fact it's the very thing they do best. They'd prefer to get in and out and *then* blow the place sky high... as they're running to the beach.

If there is one thing that will put a silver bullet in your disappearing act, it's blabbing about your old life.

"I sure showed the IRS! Those turkeys won't bother me ever again!" you say just a little too loudly in Bangkok, piquing the interest of a former IRS tax agent a few stools down.

Bottom line: You should value your new identity as though it were your life, because, well, it is. Treat it as such. Loose lips and all.

Restrict Physical Access

Never trust anyone with your laptop overseas. If you loan it out, ensure you're there as they use it.

Inside your laptop lies the heart and soul of your business. Break it off with a vengeful Thai girl and she can do a lot more than just the battery-acid-to-the-face on the other girl. She can **ruin** you. Thus, you must encrypt your operating system. You needn't go as far as Bin Laden did and avoid laptops altogether, but you need to be aware that comfort breeds mistakes, and costly ones at that.

If you're a freelancer, an author, or just have an online side hustle, guard your passwords and pen names like they were the keys to Heaven itself. Never give too many details, especially to strangers.

Last thing you want is a string of bad (fake) reviews from every one of her Thai brothers calling you a white hot ball of canine terror who plagiarizes and eats freckled pigtailed girls.

Want to stay invisible? Don't give out your last name.

Preserve Your Reputation

Ever watch Game of Thrones? I did, right up until they offed poor Ned at the end of Season 1. But a line from Tyrell stuck with me: A Lannister always pays his debts. So should you. And no I don't mean your student loans. I mean debts to friends and family and other alliances, other businesses. Local, unpaid debts make enemies *fast*. Enemies can poor a can of puke-yellow paint all over your invisibility act. Imagine poor Bilbo standing there in front of all those guests covered in yellow goop.

Cut Them Loose

This means cutting loose someone who is unstable and detrimental to your stability - the same stability you worked hard to obtain. Financially unstable people tend to borrow without asking. Mentally unstable people tend to embarrass and stalk until you until your house is burning down to the riff of Ozzy.

This requires saying no. In some cases it requires *firing* someone in your life who makes a lot of noise flapping their gums (remember Bin Laden's courier?). A maid with sticky fingers, too, can be catastrophic, but still easier to fire than your live-in girlfriend. Better to suffer a bruised ego for a day than lose a business... and clients.

When I dated a filipina in Dumaguete, it was expected of me to bring a gift to her brother's birthday party. She wanted me to buy him an Ipad. I nearly choked to death on my cashews.

"Can't you afford it?" she slyly asked. "Sure can. But I'm not your white ATM," I sternly replied.

I hurt her feelings, true enough, but spared myself the expense of buying all her relatives electronic gadgets that cost $300-400 per item on all future social engagements. Later I found this to be common no matter where one is in the Philippines. They all think you're rich if you are there since a plane ticket costs an arm and a leg.

Yep, if you can pay a grand for a ticket to Asia, you're rich buddy. Bill Gates rich.

Risky Friendships

When you are a stranger in a strange land, it can be tempting to accept any and all friendships that fall into your lap. You've got a shiny new identity. You feel more alive than ever before. No debts. No criminal past. No angry ex looking to string you up from the nearest tree if you don't fork over two grand by the end of the month.

Then you meet someone at a convention and offer a beer after you forge a connection. He smiles with a row of perfect teeth. Nods and hmms and offers expert marketing advice. You think, "Gee, this guy appears to be intelligent and business-minded. I like him. Could make for a decent business partner."

After all, you could always use more clients as a digital nomad, right? Only later you find out he runs a tranny dating website for Thais and wants you to "meet someone to discuss better ways to attract clientele."

I'm sure you know the risks of such a scenario.

SNOWDEN'S MISTAKES

Edward Snowden.

The man is an interesting character study as to how far a single human will go on personal ethics alone.

He had insisted from the very beginning that he believed the NSA's surveillance programs to be in violation of the U.S. Constitution, and that the people who founded that Constitution ought to know about them. Nothing good, he said, ever came from keeping tax-funded programs in the dark from the taxpayers themselves.

He also claimed that he never intended to hide his identity (after running of course). What can we learn from his mistakes? What not to do if we decide to disappear?

Mistake #1: Moscow

It was WikiLeaks founder Julian Assange that provided for Snowden's stay in Hong Kong, even recommending that he not go to South America on account of the physical danger to himself. Not that the place is paradise since the general instability of the area makes for a miserable experience in a lot of cities, cartels included.

So as luck would have it, he ended up in Russia when his passport was yanked.

And it isn't even what Snowden *said* that is most appealing to the Russians. Rather, it's what he did not say - those unwritten, unspoken matrix of secrets that are a veritable *gold mine* for Russian Intelligence. It's a good bet that if Washington ever offers him a plea deal and allows him back on American soil, we will see the same stalling behavior we saw with Putin's decision. They'll not give him up so easily. Quite the catch-22.

Mistake #2: One Passport

With the kind of security clearance Edward had, getting a second passport in a country friendly to the United States should have been easy peasy. Yes, said country would certainly have handed him over, but not without at least a delay that might have granted him more time. The U.S. government will know it if you do, but it is not a foregone conclusion that they would be revoked simultaneously. If that were the case, we'd all be living under One Government by now (Thank Heaven for small miracles).

Mistake 3: Facetime

Facetime kills anonymity quicker than anything else. This nail in the coffin had a two prong effect: The first being that of honesty. Snowden could address the American public without there being any doubt to the validity of his identity. If he'd stayed anonymous, he'd have always struggled with proving who he was and that his words rung true.

The mistake of course comes in on that second effect: The FBI now knew his face. Eventually the NSA would have nailed him even if he hadn't gone public, but it might have given him more time since Snowden's appeal could very well have dragged out any extradition request.

Takeaway: Don't flee to a country that will do you more harm than the country you are fleeing *from*. True, we see Edward as living a somewhat normal, if modest life in that sprawling ex-Soviet country... but that life may one day be short lived.

When the dust settles, and the interviews by comedians cease, and we no longer hear of Snowden or WikiLeaks, we might just have missed the disappearing act of Putin deciding to be a little more forceful in gaining access to that vault of secrets between Edward's ears. Don't let that be you.

DEFEATING FACIAL RECOGNITION TECHNOLOGY

I'm not Spiderman, and I'd wager you're not Quicksilver from the X-Men (mutant kid who can run 200mph and push bullets around like Skittles).

Let's be honest for a moment. I don't care for the government using much of any kind of facial-scan technology to measure how many steps it takes me to go to the gym or if I'm whistling a copyrighted tune out of my backside after eating a bowl of Chocolate Frosted Sugar Bombs.

Nor can I (legally, anyway) take a double-bladed axe to all of the traffic cams in the city where I live. So what *can* I do? What can *you* do?

First off, let's not panic since we have some credible legal options. Let's also discuss what it is and what it is not and where it is going to be a decade out.

Facial recognition is not Star Trek technology, nor is it a perfect way to spot a kidnapper or merely spy on Uncle Frick. And rest assured that for the rest of us, there are flaws that can be exploited. When you hear about facial recognition technology such as that used by social networks, what they really refer to is the techniques used to identify a photo or a moving face in a reel of film. The algorithms target spacial differences and anomalies along your face: how far the chin protrudes, how far the eyes are apart, the biometrics of the ears and so forth. Does she have Asian features? Russian cheekbones and nose? Indonesian lips? There are almost a hundred nodes along a human face for an algorithm to work with. That doesn't sound so bad.

Only the bad news is that it only takes 20 or so nodes relative to a man or woman's face to be identified. If a satellite can identify a person's brand of shoe from low orbit, you can imagine how easy it would be to size up a person's face and match that with a database.

The good news is that even mathematical algorithms can be tricked. Take Google for example. Google spends billions on its algorithms and much less on its programmers, which coincidentally happen to be some of the best on Earth, yet it is often simple techniques blackhat marketers use to fool the engine into thinking data is relevant when it really isn't. A false positive, to say. Google coders adapt the code. The blackhatters catch on. Word spreads around the hive mind and they adapt as well.

Look At Your Feet

Alex Kilpatrick is a facial-recognition expert and research leader at the TIS (Tactical Info Systems) in Texas. He did an interview for the BBC where he talked about simple ways to defeat these systems. One being: Look at your feet. This obscures your identity in ways the cameras can't account for. And yes, you guessed right if you said the homeless have the advantage here.

When I was a student at Loyola University in New Orleans, donating my plasma kept my belly full on a few hard months as I awaited the arrival of my student loan check. Lots of students did this. Selling plasma was like selling gold when you were starving and I could think of a lot of other bodily fluids that might prove embarrassing to sell.

Well as fate would have it, I had to bus it down to the plasma center once when my car engine went kaput. Buses in New Orleans were something I absolutely *dreaded*. I had to walk a block or so down Canal Street, aka Bum Central. It was an educational walk.

But it was no short walk. And I recall bringing my psychology book along on the RTA route to kill time. I'd occasionally look up, grinning at how in sync the bums and winos walks would be: Jazzy yet almost in tune with each other.

You've seen it no doubt... Head down over a long beard, shotglass of bourbon and swaggering. I came to admire them for their stealthy way of blending into the trashy panoramic atmosphere. The entire street had several theaters back then and I'd see them hawk and hork and spit and panhandle and all the while barely raising their eyes to speak to honest Johns. Some of them even wore sunglasses.

Sunglasses Don't Work

Perhaps a few bums wanted to be trendy bums. But the problem with wearing shades in order to fool surveillance cams is that the algorithm will simply ignore that section of your face and focus more intensely on other parts of it. In fact I'd say judging from the research done by the Chinese on facial recognition systems, it doesn't matter how big the glasses are, either.

Obnoxious Clothing DOES Work

If you've got a few articles of clothing with pictures of other people's faces on it, that will disrupt the algorithm in the same way billboards disrupt Google Earth's Street View algorithm that tries to smear real people's faces on the street for privacy.

Clothing like this:

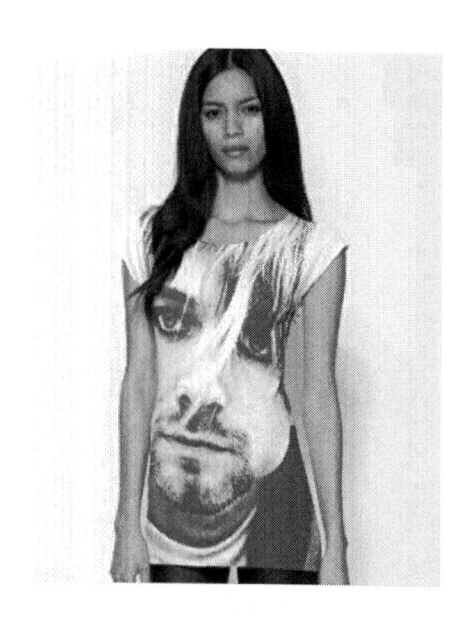

Or this:

You don't necessarily need to go with a "face shirt" either, but the image below is probably a stretch for society to accept:

Helmets

Speaking of what society tolerates and what it doesn't, a beard and hat disguise is probably better than wearing a helmet for too long. A friend of mine remarked that he wears a full-face helmet whenever he rides a Ninja. Keeps the bugs out of his hair, he says, but when he tries to pump gasoline while wearing it, the gas attendant won't turn on the pumps until he takes it *off*.

Well, no wet-behind-the-ears teenager is going to tell him what to do, so off he goes to another gas station. An Exxon this time. The end result: Same thing. He found out that the owners of these gas stations like to have a biker's face on the camera in case the police come by asking about a kidnapped little girl.

IR LEDs

Remember that what facial recognition systems zero-in on is *relative triangles*, such as the tip of your nose to the bottom of your chin and over to your ears, or from your chin to your forehead and over to your eyes. You're unique in this way just as your fingerprints are unique. No two people are the same.

But an IR LEDs will disrupt this greatly. We discussed laser pointers disrupting instruments on jets. Well the same principle applies here, and I predict this will find its way into our clothing styles in the coming years whether we like it or not, depending on how invasive Big Brother's systems become in the next decade.

The downside is that it doesn't work unless everyone is doing it since by using this you will clearly stand out on a monitor. Some celebrities used to wear/use these to discourage the paparazzi whenever they'd come sniffing. It was set off by a camera flash and the results were not quite what they'd hoped.

Then again, the antivirus company AVG is reportedly working on so-called "invisibility glasses" that thwart facial software altogether. It uses LEDs that move around the eyes and nose which distort any images the system takes for the purpose of recognizing you.

Unfortunately it's only in the beginning stages at this point, but I believe this is only the tip of the iceberg. Can Frodo's elvish cloak be far behind?

College Dorms

These are the absolute *worst* for privacy. At Loyola University during my junior year, I as well as every other resident of the Cabra Hall residence had to show our IDs every single time we entered to the desk attendant. It didn't matter if we'd spoken to said attendant a thousand times that day or (heaven forbid) we were related to her. Neither did it matter if we swiped the card without an error.

Nope. Every single time we walked through the front double-steel doors to that fortress of doom, we got the "Papers please!" spiel.

Only one time the grad student behind the dusty counter caught me on a bad day after a hard rain and a failed calculus test, and I refused. For a nanosecond I even considered flipping her off. But no, that'd too rude even for me as well as granting her that power of attention she craved. So I just walked right by her as though I'd swallowed an invisibility potion.

She didn't like that, and the next time I came around at dinnertime about 7 o'clock, she lashed out at me with a few insults she'd brewed in my absence. Not only that, her face changed right before my eyes, going from conservative librarian girl with glasses and cinnamon latte to a gorgon's daughter looking for fresh meat.

That was it. I got pretty steamed myself and so I frisbeed the ID at her like that feral kid with the boomerang in Road Warrior - so fast I thought it'd put her eye out. It struck her forehead dead center before flipping away, over her desk and down her arm and into her bookbag. Next thing I knew I'm in the resident manager's office justifying my terrorist-like actions. But more shocking than this was that he had my midterm grades on a Matrix-green computer screen in front of him.

I didn't enjoy sitting it out a semester.

CHARTING A NEW COURSE

It could be that you want to disappear for non-criminal reasons. You don't have any debt. You simply want to get away to start a new chapter in life. Wipe the soul-draining high school slate clean and build anew. Become a French artist. Maybe a trainer of wind surfers in Bora Bora, watching fire dancers twirl flame every night as the sun sinks down while three filipinas you've never met are eying you up and down from the water.

Maybe you want to be a boat tour guide in the Philippines that brings all the newly minted expats out to see the whale feedings while exotic filipinas coo over your white skin (I saw with my own eyes how obsessed filipinas are with with this - entire aisles in pharmacies filled with skin-whitening products.)

Memories often make the man, but if you get rid of the things, that is, the settings, the people, the jobs, the polluted air, that miserable dragon-breathing boss named Winona who works in HR, well you just have no idea *what* gifts await you on the other side. Just do it.

It's not the things we did in life that we regret on our death beds, but the things we never took up. Those procrastinations that we kept waving back into the horizon, over and over, never taking action. Forever leaving it to *some other guy* to step out of the safe zone.

When I lived in a small town in Louisiana many years ago, I kept running into old girlfriends. Old high school chums. Old sluts. Old memories that dragged me down like the girl I'd never asked out who was now the woman in the red dress, a wall survivor now hitched to the mayor.

Life's little moments like these made a habit of creeping up on me like a flow of lava does a small sleepy town in Hawaii. Moments that I never thought I'd be reminded of day in, day out, slowly devouring me like lava embers do straw huts. Slow at first, warm before the embrace, but when the hit, well. They melt any sense of adventure.

So I made a break for a clean slate. First to Canada, then to SE Asia.

Don't just *dream* about the clean slate. Take action. Meditating on your dreams, as I've discovered, can actually prevent them from becoming reality. It's suboptimal to meditate on the end results - You sipping margaritas in Bora Bora. That only works if you meditate on taking active steps towards making the dream happen in the first place. So don't meditate on the end-result...You must visualize yourself *working toward the dream*, mixing the reagents that, when all is said and done, is powerful enough to give you wings.

Are you a writer? Visualize yourself writing at the keyboard, banging out five thrilling novels per year, or making six figures by building an insanely good client base as a copywriter.

AFTERWORD

A tough question I repeatedly asked myself when I was overseas was this: Am I still the same person in Dumaguete that I was in New Orleans? What about Toronto, Canada?

I mean I acted the same, very laid back and easy to approach, almost too easy now that I think about it. I ate the same - a good Mexican restaurant with cheese enchiladas and salsa with a side of guacamole with Blue Bell Homemade Vanilla ice cream for dessert. I even smelled the same - Midnight and Noir cologne since the day they arrived.

Though no Mardi Gras or beignets were anywhere to be found in the Phils, I still believed in the same God. I'd not really disappeared so much as just teleported, I feared, just as Nightcrawler did in so many comics, escaping doom.

Truly becoming invisible, I found, involved throwing out old grudges, grudges that rot the spirit and the mind. Grudges, I later found, that not only cause ulcers but rot any sense of risk or adventure. We're explorers and we don't like being anchored too far from shore without a rowboat. We like safety. We like security. But sometimes you must throw caution to the wind and swim for it completely naked... yes, even with sharks lurking about. And it is this unknown (How many sharks? What kind? Meat-o-sauruses?) that keeps so many would-be explorers at bay.

The key to overcoming your fear is courage. Well, that and a little imagination.

Envision yourself as someone else, say, a storyteller like Bilbo Baggins, tired of the retched relatives squawking like harpies over who gets what if he croaks one midsummer night. Bilbo the wanderer. Bilbo the *explorer*.

You have sufficient gold to navigate every hillside, every culture, every dragon's den. You can visit South Korea and meet the most beautiful people on Earth and all with a clean slate since no one knows of your mistakes. Where every moment is now, where you are invisible, yet visible. Tokyo, Thailand, Philippines, it's all yours for the taking. Your new face will go a long way in those parts of the world.

So go and take action to make it real!

CONCLUSION

Here we are at the end of our journey. Thank you for sticking it through to the end. Hopefully it wasn't too painful.

If you liked the information in this book or found it entertaining, then please take a moment to leave a review so others can learn to protect themselves from Big Brother, tyranny and other evil-minded taffers who dislike freedom and individual choice - and think bureaucrats can make better decisions than you can.

May God Bless and Keep You On Life's Journey!

Made in the USA
Middletown, DE
20 January 2018